GONE WITH THE SUGAR

How I Lost 106 Pounds In 7 Months Just By Cutting Out Sugar!

First Edition

ISBN: 9781796663709

Limit of Liability

Dedication

I want to dedicate this book to my family. I'm sorry. I didn't know at the time about sugar and the damage I was causing to my family. What I thought was love was addiction. When I think about the role sugar played in your lives I'm saddened, but I pray going forward you'll let me help you become more aware of sugar.

I want to thank my Lord Jesus Christ for saving me and giving me a purpose.

"Don't do anything for selfish purposes but with humility think of others as better than yourselves."

Philippians 2:3

Table of Contents

Change Your Life Before Sugar Takes Your Life 1

My Journey in Numbers 6

What I wish I knew then 8

Remember The Fundamentals And You Don't Need To Follow A Strict Diet Plan ... 10

The Only Four Rules Of Keto That Matter 11

What's The Big Deal About Sugar? 15

How Much Total Sugar Do You Need? 17

Note on Artificial Sweeteners 19

How To Cut Through The Fog And Find What's Important In Those Nutrition Labels.
.... 21

Sugar Disguises 24

Flavor Blends Listed As A Top Three Ingredient 25

Package Labeling Tricks 26

Common Sources of Hidden Sugar 28

Cigarettes 30

Alcohol 31

How Anyone Can Adopt This Lifestyle Regardless Of Budget Or Life Circumstances
.... 33

Yeah, yeah. I've tried every fad diet out there. How's this going to be any different?
.... 33

Come on! I'm just way too busy to cook healthy meals three times a day. 33

This sounds like a rich girl's diet. I work for a living. I can't afford to eat like this.
.... 34

How To Overcome Withdrawal Symptoms 35

Tips for Lasting Success 40

1) Trusting yourself is good, but control is better. 40

2) Stick to a food budget. 40

3) Always keep a healthy snack on hand. 42

4) Partner with someone 42

5) Keep good notes in a journal. 42

6) Buy specialty ingredients in bulk. 42

7) Adjust your routine..42

How To Avoid Sugar When Eating Out...43

Miscellaneous Money Saving Tips...44

How To Create Tasty, Sugar Free Versions Of Any Recipe 46

Natural Sugar Substitutes 46

How to Work With Gluten-Free Flour Blends 47

Natural Starchy Carbohydrate Replacements 49

    Almond Flour...49

    Garbanzo Bean Flour (Chickpeas)..49

    Oat Fiber (not to be confused with oat flour) 49

    Coconut flour 50

    Lupin beans Flour 50

    Green banana flour 50

Use Cauliflower or jicama instead of potatoes 50

Sample One Week Meal Plan 51

Meal plan day 1 51

Meal plan day 2 51

Meal plan day 3 52

Meal plan day 4 52

Meal plan day 5 52

Meal plan day 6 53

Meal plan day 7 53

Recipes...54

Breakfast...55

Eggs Florentine Biscuit W/ Ham & Cheese 55

Breakfast Tortilla Wrap 56

Baked cauliflower Grits casserole 57

Breakfast Grits Bowl 58

Cheese and Ham Cup – Microwaveable...59

Egg Spinach Bacon Breakfast Sandwich 60

Biscuit W/ Ham & Cheese...61

Spinach Mushroom Cheese Omelet...62

Spicy Breakfast Wrap 63

Scrambled Eggs with Collards 64

Green Banana Flour Waffles/Pancakes 65

Shrimp and Cauliflower grits 66

Oat Fiber Pancake recipe 67

Almond Flour Muffins 68

Microwavable cheddar bacon biscuits 69

Homemade Biscuits 70

Biscuits and Gravy 71

Breakfast Cauliflower squares 72

Raspberry Danish 73

Soups 75

Cauliflower Soup 75

Chicken Noodle Soup 76

Hot "potato" collard soup 77

Kale Chicken Noodle soup 78

Broccoli Cheddar Soup with Ham and Bacon 79

White sauce Sausage Kale Chili 80

Crock pot sauerkraut soup 81

Breads, Wraps and Pizza Crusts 82

Almond Flour Bread gluten free 82

Oat Fiber Bread gluten free 83

Gluten-Free Hamburger Buns 84

Spinach and Flax Wraps gluten free 85

Ultra-Low Carb Tortillas 86

Cauliflower Crust For Any Type of Pizza 87

Radish Crust White Pizza – 0 sugar, 1 carb 88

Deep Dish prosciutto basil Pizza 89

Mashed Cauliflower to Replace Mashed Potatoes 91

Sides 92

grits bowl 92

Simple Fake Potato salad 93

Green tomato chutney 94

Broccoli Stir-Fry 95

Collard Greens 96

Jicama (potatoe) Salad 97

Au graten jicama 98

Spinach stuffed baked mushrooms 99

Salads 100

Baked chicken salad 100

Entrees (Lunches, Brunches and Dinners) 101

Cauliflower Crust Buffalo Chicken Blue cheese pizza 101

Chicken and Dumplings with Einkorn flour 103

Enchiladas 105

Low Carb Spaghetti 106

Healthy Fried Chicken 107

Tamale/ Enchilada/ Taco Meat 109

Quesadillas with Pork 110

Pork Fried Rice 111

Meatloaf 112

Rice and chicken 113

Puréed Radish with Ham and Swiss Cheese Bake 114

Cauliflower and ham bake 115

Salmon patties 116

Sausage Kale Jicama one pot meal 117

Beef stew 118

Microwave Shrimp and shiritake rice casserole 119

Chicken and rice 120

Mashed Jicama potatoes recipe 121

Raspberry Birch custard kuchen 122

Oven Fried green tomatoes 123

Condiments 124

Ranch Dressing 124

Creamy Avocado Dressing 125

Red Onion Blueberry Dressing / Glaze 126

Creamy Italian dressing / glaze 127

Pecan Vinaigrette salad dressing / marinade 128

Spinach dip chilled or baked 129

Horseradish sauce 130

Bourbon BBQ sauce 131

Ketchup 132

Mayonnaise 133

Marinara sauce 134

Maple Syrup 135

Sugar-Free jelly 136

Sugar-Free orange marmalade 137

Snacks 138

Hot Wings - 0 Sugar, 0 Carb 138

Chicken Skin Black pepper sea salt Chips – 0 Sugar, 0 Carb 139

Pork skin nachos (microwave or oven) 0 sugar, 0 carb 140

Microwave cheese chips 141

Cheese chips with chia seeds 142

Strawberry Cream spread 143

Microwave Flaxseed crackers 144

Salted caramel pecans 145

Sugar-Free Donut Holes 146

CAKE POP MAKER DIRECTIONS 147

Microwavable Single Serve Brownie 149

Microwavable Banana Nut Cake 150

Microwave Vanilla Cake with Chocolate Ganache 152

Desserts 153

Chocolate Chip Cookie 153

Peanut Butter Cookie 154

Microwave butter mints 155

Garbanzo bean flour chocolate chip cookies 156

Butter Cookies 157

Coconut Flour "Sugar" Cookies 158

Chewy Chocolate Chip Cookies 159

Peanut Butter Fudge 160

Blueberry Cake with icing.. 161

Pecan Fudge.. 162

Cheesecake 0 carb 0 sugar 163

Fudge with walnuts... 164

About the Author 165

Change Your Life Before Sugar Takes Your Life

I'm the last person in the world anyone ever expected to preach a healthy lifestyle, but August 1, 2017 was a day of awakening for me. My husband and I were driving home from our family reunion and I was pouring through the pictures. I did not like what I saw. Nor did I like the way I felt about myself. I was very overweight. I was obese!

My birthday was also a little more than a week away. I was determined not to go another year looking and feeling the way I did. I was sick and tired of being sick and tired. So, I started looking on the internet for yet another diet.

The next day we learned one of our cousins passed away. Her passing was unexpected. She too was overweight, and I believe this played a part in her early death. I realize that if I did not improve my health, I too might die… much sooner than I would like. I reflected on my family and how much I love them. I was now more determined to lose weight and get healthy. Little did I know the reverse would happen… by getting healthy, I lost the weight!

I started looking on the internet for yet another diet. Instead, I came across several videos explaining the dangers of sugar and how it acts just like a drug. After watching those videos, I realized I was an addict. Just how much of an addict? Pretty big! Literally!

For example, instead of a coffee addiction, I needed several tall glasses of ultra-sweet Southern iced tea every day, or else I was a grumpy mess. I would make sugar-laden meals for my family and bake irresistible sweets on a daily basis. I was a manufacturer's rep for some of the largest candy companies for years. Or more like a street dealer, if we're being honest. I hustled sugar to adults and kids alike. Even offering free samples to get them hooked.

This may be a controversial claim that skinny doctors in lab coats scoff at and mutter, "Oh, the results are inclusive," but they don't know what was going through my mind. I was psychologically and physically dependent on sugar. I needed my fix and escape just the same as any alcoholic or chain smoker. Substance abuse runs deep in my family's genes, so I'm sorry to say I'm quite familiar with the signs.

Good times, bad times. Stressed or relaxed, sugar was my drug of choice. It was my crutch and my enslaver. It controlled my thoughts, actions and moods. If I wasn't eating or drinking sugar, I was counting down the seconds until I could.

The more I read and researched, the more I began to understand how addictive sugar is and how it's hidden everywhere. Now I know many doctors and researchers clear their throats at this point and interrupt with, "*Actually*, sugar is only a problem in excessive doses."

But excessive sugar intake is the problem. Who really comes close to taking in a moderate dose of sugar a day? A typical fast food combo meal (burger, large fries and large soda) from any of the big chain joints consists of 90-120 grams of added sugar. Just with lunch, you've busted your recommended daily sugar intake of 25 grams for women and 38 for men several times over. And that's the obvious stuff.

Even if you're steering clear of junk food and do your best to get some exercise every day, take a peek at your belly. If you're frustrated because your spare tire keeps growing or your hips keep widening no matter what you do, I guarantee that's because you're unknowingly wolfing down hundreds of calories in unneeded empty carbs every day. All of which your body is storing up as fat for safekeeping.

Processed added sugar is present in 74% of the items in a typical grocery store,[1] mostly hidden behind odd chemical names that don't explicitly state that they're a sugar. Ultra-processed things like maltodextrin, fruit juice concentrate or 42 HFCS (aka high fructose corn syrup) that are actually higher on the glycemic index than table sugar.

I'll show you how to quickly spot this camouflaged poison in the next chapter, but right now let the shear scope of the sugar epidemic sink in. Everything from canned vegetables to diet snacks ("low sugar" is not an FDA regulated claim, so it means whatever the manufacturer wants) are packed full of added sugar, on top of the natural sugars. Sometimes for the sake of preservation, but mostly to make their products more addictively sweet so you keep craving and buying ever more.

Even if someone is working out, they're still wolfing down more calories from secret sugar than they're burning on an average day. For example, a 200-pound woman going for a 30-minute jog will burn between 300-400 calories in her workout.[2] Pretty impressive, but if she's like most Americans, she's consuming between 100-200 grams of extra secret sugar above and beyond the recommended daily limit.[3] With four calories included per gram of sugar, that's 400-800 pointless calories she's taking in every single day! Despite all the exercise, she just can't win and keeps packing on pounds no matter what. Is it any wonder that 71% of Americans are overweight or obese?[4] In fact, 40% of Americans meet the clinical definition of obesity (including myself for most of my life).

---

[1] Ng, S.W., Slining, M.M., & Popkin, B.M. (2012). "Use of caloric and noncaloric sweeteners in US consumer packaged foods, 2005-2009." *Journal of the Academy of Nutrition and Dietetics*, 112(11). Http://sugarscience.ucsf.edu/hidden-in-plain-sight/#.XGVBclxKiUk

[2] WebMd. *Exercise Calculator*. https://www.webmd.com/fitness-exercise/healthtool-exercise-calculator

[3] US Department of Agriculture. (2018). *U.S. Consumption of Caloric Sweeteners.* Tables 49-53. https://www.ers.usda.gov/data-products/sugar-and-sweeteners-yearbook-tables.aspx

[4] Gussone, F. (October 13, 2017). *America's Obesity Epidemic Reaches Record High, New Report Says*. https://www.nbcnews.com/health/health-news/america-s-obesity-epidemic-reaches-record-high-new-report-says-n810231

So why do most people not care? If researchers found any other unknown substance lurking in 74% of our foodstuffs, there would be a public panic. But not sugar. Sugar is tasty. Sugar is our friend. Sugar is our favorite addiction.

And it's fattening us up for the slaughter one hidden spoonful at a time.

There is hope though. Just go cold turkey from the sugar until you have your weight under control. Ok, obviously the practical application is a bit harder than that, but we're in this together. If I could pull this off while living in the Deep South, where sugar is basically a food group, then anyone can.

Whenever I'm feeling overwhelmed, I anchor myself by glaring at the mirror and saying, "What are you willing to give up in order to get what you need?" Be honest with yourself. When I talk to people who are addicted to sugar like I was, they tell me they need to do what I've done, but they really just mean they "want" to. It hasn't sunk in to them yet that they *need* this lifestyle change.

That's why when they hear I had to go cold turkey and I had to get rid of so many sugary items, things I thought I could never get rid of, they start to make excuses. I get it. I was one of those same people. I would always be on the lookout for the latest fad, the latest diet. The quick fix. I would pick out the easy part and say I can handle it, but when it came time to give up something I was really addicted to, I would discredit or discount the idea and not even try it. Just like an addict I wanted to keep my fix. If I had a fraction of the money I have spent over the years on diet and weight loss schemes, I could retire and travel the world.

I got rid of all the sugar in my house. The cookies, the chips, the cakes, the pies, the white sugar—everything! I went extreme. I started reading the back of packages and labels. If it had sugar in it, then it was gone. I threw out a lot of stuff and cried. Not because of the dollar value but because of the health cost I had inflicted on my family over the years.

I knew I had to quit sugar by going cold turkey. I knew it would be rough. I had no idea just how tough. Over the next three days, I had the shakes, the sweats, the mood swings. I would have to lie down with a cold wash rag on my forehead. It was unreal. It was like an alien was inside my body. My mind was trying to tell my body what to do, but my body was not cooperating. At one point, I thought I was having a heart attack. My doctor told me it was just withdrawal from sugar, similar to someone having withdrawal from drugs or alcohol. I could not believe it. Wow! I thought this must be how an addict feels. This only motivated me more to quit sugar.

After five days I was okay. I didn't crave sugar anymore. I didn't want sugar anymore. My diet over that first month wasn't anything special. It wasn't until weeks later that I learned I was even following a Keto diet. I'd yet to learn about all the great natural sugar substitutes out there, so I stuck to tried and true sugar-free foods:

- Heaps of low-carb vegetables, mostly spinach, collards, kale and anything dark green.
- Eggs have no sugar, so I splurged on them. Scrambled, boiled, fried, even poached (I learned poached eggs are not my favorite), I gobbled up several eggs every day.
- Any type of lean meat has no sugar, so you don't have to go vegan to cut out the sugar. With that excuse up my sleeve, I pigged out on beef, pork, chicken, fish and most especially bacon. I still keep a bag of bacon around as my go-to protein snack.

Sure, eating only tons of meat, eggs and green vegetables is not the optimum diet. I've since moved to a much more balanced one, but at the beginning of my "sugar detox" I was desperate for fast results. And those desperate measures yielded unbelievable results. The benefits of cutting out all sugar drastically outweighed the fact that I was eating too much fat and not exercising enough. Thankfully, I did correct those two problems later.

At the time though, I was only focused on breaking my addiction. On the same day my cravings vanished, I noticed my favorite pair of jeans slouching around my hips. I had to dig out a belt from the closet to hold them up. First time in years I'd worn a belt for a practical purpose and not just as a fashion accessory!

Again, it wasn't until later that I learned I was entering that fabled ketosis phase of the Keto diet, where your body is deprived of a steady external glucose supply and starts pillaging your fat stores for energy. I probably burned a few hundred more calories crying with joy.

Of course, now came the hard part. Staying off the drugs. Staying off sugar for good.

I grew up in the South and I still live there. I grew up on deep fried foods, sweet veggies, biscuits and cornbread, banana pudding, and all those yummy, decadent desserts. And of course, Southern sweet tea. Sugar was everywhere and in everything. If something wasn't sweet, it was animal feed.

So it was extra weird when I broke my sugar addiction. People gawked at how I would cringe if there was the slightest tinge of sugar in something, yet enjoy "boring" healthy foods, which now taste better to me. For example, when I have a blueberry, it tastes as sweet as a candy bar. But even just the scent of milk chocolate turns my stomach over. Most cheeses also have no sugar in them, yet Swiss cheese tastes sweet to me. The same for nuts.

Still, I'd say the hardest change for me was skipping dressing and sauces. It's hard and expensive to find any condiment that's truly sugar free. I could adapt to eating salads instead of fried everything, but for Pete's sakes, they're the most boring thing in the world without dressing!

So I learned to make my own sugar-free dressings… and loved the difference. Soon I was experimenting and replacing every one of my favorite recipes with sugar-free and low-carb ingredients.

I don't claim to be the world's greatest cook, but every time I coach someone on this new lifestyle, it's my sugar-free versions of popular recipes that blows their minds. These aren't expensive nor take long to prepare. Most you can whip up faster than the traditional unhealthy version. For example, I've discovered cauliflower to be one of the most versatile vegetables around. My recipes show how to use cauliflower to make pizza crust, fried rice, mashed potatoes and even mac-n-cheese. All with the same texture as the original and even a slightly sweeter taste. I can't wait to see what new substitutions my readers come up with!

Now onto what I did after I broke my sugar addiction.

I am sure there will be those who read this and judge me. But this book is not about getting people to like me. It is about sharing what worked for me so others may apply the same, or similar, tactics in their life. I was addicted to sugar and I found a way to break my addiction. To me, this was life-changing! My new addiction is leading a healthy lifestyle.

I hope you do whatever it takes to break your sugar addiction. Your life depends on it!

What are you willing to give up in order to get what you need? For me, I gave up sugar in order to get healthy and lose weight. I want everyone who reads this book to look at how much sugar is in their diet.

Where do you begin? There is so much conflicting information out there telling us what we need to be eating. It's confusing. The best advice I can give you, after cutting out the sugar, is to stay flexible. You don't have to follow any rigid diet plan, other than ruthlessly managing your sugar intake. Simply listen to your body. Cut out the sugar and see what happens with your appetite. I believe you will be quite surprised at the results. I know I was!

I declared war on sugar, and although I have won the battle, I want to win the war! In order to do so, I need to be diligent and keep looking at ingredients to make sure I do not feed my addiction. This can be difficult at times. For example, now that I have started eating out again (I did not eat out while I was breaking my sugar addiction), I need to be cautious about the ingredients used to prepare my meal. The restaurant may tell you there is no sugar in a particular menu item, or no sugar was used to prepare it, but that's not always true. The staff aren't nutritionists. They're cooks and waiters and don't have the time nor interest to do any research.

I am not embarrassed to ask questions, since my health depends on eating foods prepared with ingredients that are not HARMFUL to my body. You'll have to become a sugar detective too, just like me. But don't worry, it's not that hard. I lay out all the key things you're looking for in the "How to Cut Through the Fog" chapter.

When I started this lifestyle change, August 1, 2017, I weighed 240.4 lbs. In 7 months, I had lost 105.6 lbs. I weighed in at 134.8 lbs. on February 23, 2018. Since then, I have maintained a healthy lifestyle which has allowed me to keep the weight off. A year later, February 2019, my weight fluctuates a pound or two, but is consistently 135 lbs.

When I look at the charts showing my weight loss, I can't believe my eyes. When I look at pictures of me from the past and today, I want to cry. I feel humbled and thankful to God for my lifestyle change. And I can't wait for you to feel that way too!

My Journey in Numbers

August 1, 2017 – I weighed in at 240.4 lbs. at the start of my lifestyle change.

August 8, 2017 – After 1 week, I had lost just over 6 lbs. During this time, I had 'broken' my addiction to sugar. I wasn't sure if the weight loss would happen however, I physically felt much better.

August 15, 2017 – I weighed in at 230.8 lbs. I had lost 10 pounds in 14 days. Plus I was feeling much better about myself and my eating habits.

August 22, 2017 – I weighed in at 226.8 lbs. Just under 14 pounds in 21 days. I thought the weight loss would have been more significant by now. However, I was determined not to be deterred in my lifestyle change.

August 29, 2017 – I weighed in at 224 lbs. I had lost a total of 16.4 pounds in 4 weeks. I was slightly worried that the weight loss should have been higher, yet I was feeling so much better, both physically and emotionally.

October 3, 2017 – I weighed in at 204.8 lbs. I had lost a little over 35 pounds in 2 months. I was averaging 4 pounds weight loss per week. I did not realize it at the time, but my weight loss was consistent every week. None of the roller coast ride of losing weight and gaining it back like I had experienced on other diets.

October 31, 2017 – I weighed in at 194.8 lbs. Now I was beginning to get excited. I had lost over 45 pounds in 3 months. I was consistently losing 4 pounds a week without the roller coaster effect!

December 5, 2017 – I weighed in at 184.4 lbs. I expected my weight loss to slow during November as I did a whole lot of baking for my extended family leading up to, and for Thanksgiving. I was impressed that my weight loss continued and without the roller coaster effect. I was still excited as my total weight loss was 56 pounds over 4 months.

December 31, 2017 – At the end of the year, I weighed in at 159.4 lbs. I had lost 81 pounds over 5 months. I consistently lost 4 pounds a week without the roller coaster effect. I was excited going into the New Year and was confident my weight loss would continue.

February 23, 2018 – I weighed in at 134.8 lbs. I had lost 106 pounds in 7 months by being "Gone With The Sugar." And I felt great! Physically and Emotionally! I was winning the battle against sugar and I am more determined than ever to win the war!

When I run into people that I have not seen since I began this journey, they cannot believe it's me. One friend, whom I had not seen for over a year, could only recognize me by my eyes. As we passed in a clothing store, I said hi to her. She paused and squinted for a few seconds. "Sherry?"

Her jaw hit the floor when I hugged her. She said I was not the same person she knew. I've had similar responses from just about everyone that hadn't seen me since I began my journey. Even my doctor insisted on running tests for a tape worm. They simply couldn't believe their eyes. They would have never believed I had lost the weight and kept it off, if they had not seen me themselves.

This is hard for me to accept as a compliment. You see, I have always thought of myself as a fat person. As a child I was teased about my weight and called chubby. Although I lost 106 pounds, I still feel like that fat person inside. It's weird. But I am working on this. My mind says one thing and my body says another. As I said, I'm still working on getting the two of them together.

Surprisingly my weight loss did not involve exercise. As the weight came off, my energy level rose yet I still was not doing any form of exercise. I was no longer feeling sick and tired. I was feeling healthy and energetic. Instead of exercising, I spent most of my time researching, investigating, and creating recipes. After about five months into my lifestyle change, I finally started walking in my neighborhood. I did a few more things but as far as exercise plans, I really didn't have one. It wasn't until recently that I developed an exercise plan that will help tone and shape my body now that the weight is gone.

A word of caution: It's easy to get overwhelmed with all the information that's out there. That is why I chose one thing to change. I identified and zeroed in on sugar. I declared war on sugar. I am happy to say I have won the battle and I plan on winning the war. With that being said I don't know what my threshold, my tolerance is for sugar. Is it one candy bar, a spoonful of honey, an apple? What will cause me to fall off the wagon, so to speak. I must always be diligent and aware of how much sugar I consume. Like a drug addict getting clean and staying away from drugs, I have to avoid the temptation and stay clean… I mean stay off sugar.

In the past I thought the solution was losing weight. I thought if I lost weight, I would be healthy. Unfortunately, that only worked for a short time because I had not changed my behavior for the long term. So after losing a few pounds I would bounce back and sometimes even gain more weight. Now I know the solution was, and is, to become healthy by living a healthy lifestyle. That begins with my eating habits. Since I've dropped sugar from my diet, I have become healthy. And by becoming healthy, the weight has just melted away.

You may think this is an impossible task, much like eating an elephant. How do you eat an elephant? One bite at a time. The same goes for a healthy lifestyle. One *bite* at a time.

I have broken my sugar addiction and changed my lifestyle. Now that I am "reformed," my new addiction is to help others cut sugar from their diet and improve their lifestyle too.

I hope this book will inspire you to break your sugar addition.

Please let this book be the start of you taking control of your health before it's too late. Sugar is making us obese. Yes, not enough physical activity and eating too much fat is making us unhealthy, but sugar is the primary killer.

Over the years I had several on-going medical problems as well... plantar fasciitis, arthritis, back pain, joint pain, gastroesophageal reflux disease and diverticulitis, to name a few. After becoming "Gone With The Sugar," I no longer have issues with any of these problems.

My skin cleared up. My brain cleared up. My energy level went up. Even my eye sight improved! Maybe I should change the name of this book to up, up and away.

I hope I'm doing a good enough job of explaining and showing you how great I feel now that I have broken my sugar addiction and changed my life.

What I wish I knew then

People always ask me, "What do you know now that you wish you knew when you began?"

Oh, where to begin?

The main thing I've learned is just how much sugar had been controlling my life. I've had an addiction to sugar for years. Maybe even since birth, which is scary considering I am now in my 50's.

I was born into a backwoods family that, shall we say, fully embraced the rich food traditions of the Louisiana Bayou and rural Florida. I was always around sugary foods, sweets and beverages. I remember one time as a child having a "tea party" with my friends. In the South, this means Southern sweet tea. Even as a youngster, you knew that tea was basically just a flavor of sugar. But this time, we were out of sugar in the kitchen. So I went out to the barn. There I found a stack of 25 lb. bags of sugar. My father was a beekeeper at the time and the sugar was food for the bees during the winter. I wasn't concerned about the bees. I only cared about my tea. So I broke open a bag and got my sugar. I knew I would pay dearly for that little stunt later but at the time, I scored my sugar fix and so did my friends. That was all that mattered.

Over the years I learned to cook not from directions on a box, but from my mom, my aunt and probably the greatest teacher of all: desperation. When I was a teenaged girl, our family went through some hard times. There were some evenings when I had to whip up supper out of nothing. My parents would disappear all night without leaving any food in the house. So my younger sister and I gathered vegetables from the garden while my brothers hunted rabbits or squirrels in the woods. If we were lucky. Sometimes they only brought back frogs and small alligators. The boys hadn't eaten all day, so they weren't picky and just killed the first thing they saw. Of course, this is all a fad paleo diet nowadays, but back then we didn't feel so hip. But there was one friend we had throughout the bad times: an endless supply of sugar to sprinkle over anything to make it taste good.

While life got better, that sugar crutch never left me. As an adult I took pride in creating wonderful meals for my family and incredible desserts. At family gatherings and reunions, I would find myself in the kitchen, helping to make incredible dishes and desserts… all with sugar and always trying to outdo myself.

So you see, I'm not just talking about stress eating or binge eating (of course I did this too). Did I tell you about the time I baked a cake, ate it completely and then baked another so my family would not know?

You'll break the bonds that bind you, but we will all spend the rest of our lives battling sugar. Why? Because it has infected every corner of our food supply. Companies make billions every year hiding sugar behind different names in their products to feed our addictions and their profits. All while funding industry "think tanks" that blame obesity and diabetes solely on fat and not exercising enough.[5] So needless to say, simply breaking your sugar addiction isn't enough. You'll always have to be on guard for all those sneaky names for sugar and the labeling tricks companies will use to add sugar to their products.

I pray this book will spark something and make people look at the amount of sugar they are consuming. If this book does nothing else than inspire people to become sugar detectives and cut through the fog of the nutrition label, then it will have all been worth it.

Sugar has robbed me of my youth and much of my health over the years. But now I am healthier at 54 than I was at 30, and that is totally because I am "gone with the sugar!"

---

[5] O'Connor, Anahad. (September 12, 2016). "How the Sugar Industry Shifted Blame to Fat." *The New York Times.* Https://www.nytimes.com/2016/09/13/well/eat/how-the-sugar-industry-shifted-blame-to-fat.html

Remember The Fundamentals And You Don't Need To Follow A Strict Diet Plan

You know, the first time I heard about the Keto diet was weeks after I'd already cut out all sugar and switched to low-carb/high protein foods. Now, I never planned anything or followed any system. I just waved goodbye to the sugar and simple starches, then let my body eat whatever it craved. Basically I stumbled into Keto by accident.

One day I was chatting with a coworker and she wanted to know my "secret" to shedding pounds so fast. What diet was I using? Naturally, I didn't have a name for it, so I just explained my simple rules on what foods to avoid. After a minute, she clucked her tongue and waved her hand. "Ah, you're doing Keto. Get the body to burn fat for energy instead of glucose? I tried that once, but it was expensive and so time consuming. Everything has sugar in it. There's just no way to avoid it."

I didn't know what she was talking about but didn't want to correct her. Clearly my diet wasn't the same thing as she meant, because I was spending less time cooking and fewer dollars at the grocery store than I ever had before.

So I researched the keto program more and found everyone complaining about the same things. There were so many rules. So many "never do's" and "always do's," many of which contradicted each other. As I read up on it, I couldn't believe how complicated all the certified nutrition "gurus" were making this. I mean, it's just a diet, not a religion.

For example, you can have some sugar, just only after you've reached a healthy body weight. And instead of trying to remember an endless list of what's safe to eat and what's not, why not just figure how to replace the sugar and high carb ingredients in any recipe?

The more rules any lifestyle has, the better the chance you're going to "fall off the wagon" at some point. Flexibility in a diet isn't a weakness, but rather the key to long-term, sustainable success.

Now here's where everyone tends to get impatient and asks me how much my "program" costs.

To be fair, I thought about doing that. About intentionally overcomplicating the keto lifestyle so folks will throw their money at me to solve the problem. You know, the classic "create a problem and sell the solution" scheme that's endemic throughout the health and wellness industry.

But I don't have the time nor interest to sell you some lose-weight-quick scheme or an X day diet/detox plan. I know that's precisely what most people want. They want a pre-packaged solution, that only takes cash and not sweat to change their life. But we all know that's a waste of time and money.

Instead, I'm trying to teach you a flexible, cheap and sustainable way to adjust your lifestyle for permanent weight loss while drastically improving your quality of life. The

lessons I've learned the hard way. This "program" only ends the day you die, which statistically will be delayed by several years if you can simply keep your weight under control.[6]

While the final results are radical, no single guideline is extreme. That's the great thing about this lifestyle change: it's infinitely adaptable. You don't have to memorize a long list of "safe" and "dangerous" foods. Or go out and spend a bunch of money on special ingredients or slave away the rest of your life in the kitchen.

Most of the tips in this book are optional. They're guidelines, rather than rules. Your finances, health goals and life circumstances will change over time, so it's crucial that your healthy eating plan can adapt as well. There are only four hard and fast rules that you need to keep in mind to be truly "gone with the sugar" and thrive no matter what life throws at you.

The Only Four Rules Of Keto That Matter

1) If you're overweight, cut out *all* sugars immediately until you've reached a body mass level you're comfortable with.

Not just added or processed sugar, but everything, including natural sugars (like fruit juice) and starches (potatoes, rice, noodles, etc). This process won't take long though. Without the constant stream of external sugars pouring in, your body will cannibalize your fat stores several times faster than you could burn fat through any physical exercise.

2) Once you're at a healthy weight, you can have some sugar and simple starches while still keeping the weight off. It's all about moderation.

Aim for no more than 25 grams (6 teaspoons) of sugar a day if you're a woman and 38 grams (9 teaspoons) for men, from both natural and artificial sources. However, this is an average over time, so some days you can exceed that level as long as you compensate by cutting way back the next day. For example, say on the weekends you're extra active and really working up a sweat, so you can go right up against the max dietary guidelines of 50 grams for women and 76 grams for men. Then during the workweek when you're more sedentary you should aim for as little sugar as possible.

3) Keep track of carbs as much as sugar and avoid high-carb foods, even if you're not on a general low-carb diet. This doesn't have to be complicated though.

First, watching carbs is the only way to find those camouflaged "non-sugar sugars," such as maltodextrin. This is a common form of *uber* sweet carbohydrates (with a 60%

---

[6] Borrell, L., Samuel, L. (2014). *Body Mass Index Categories and Mortality Risk in US Adults: The Effect of Overweight and Obesity on Advancing Death.* *H*ttps://www.ncbi.nlm.nih.gov/pmc/articles/PMC3953803/

higher glycemic score than table sugar) that doesn't legally have to be labelled as sugar. You can't even count on finding maltodextrin in the ingredient list because some companies mix it into a "seasoning blend" with a healthy sounding name. So the only red flag you'll see that this or a similar fake sugar has been added is noticing a small sugar per serving rate but massive total carb count on the nutrition label.

Second, remember that even complex carbohydrates will eventually be broken down into sugar by your body. Exactly how fast it's converted and how much that sugar affects your blood sugar level are determined by the food's glycemic index. So it's crucial to count these carbs side by side with your sugar budget, or else you're ignoring the majority of your sugar intake.

But don't make it complicated. Now, there's nothing wrong with checking the glycemic index of each food item you're taking in and running the numbers to see how much sugar that translates into, but that's not really necessary. Because if you're looking for rapid weight loss, you're going to be avoiding as many carbs as possible, regardless of the glycemic index. And if you're already at a healthy weight, then there's a ton of wiggle room in the carb budget.

The official dietary guidelines say that your total carbohydrates should provide 45 to 65 percent of your daily calorie intake. So if you're following a 2000-calorie diet, then you can have between 225-325 grams of carbs per day. This is a grand total that includes all carbohydrates, such as natural sugar, added sugar and both soluble and insoluble fiber.

However, we're eliminating added sugars and minimizing natural sugars to just 25 or 38 grams a day. You can also ignore carbs from dietary fiber in your total carb tracking, since these can't be broken down by your digestive enzymes. There's a lot of room to suck in a few extra carbs without busting your sugar diet, so you don't have to stress and worry about every gram you're consuming. Personally, I follow a low carb diet and keep my average total daily carbohydrates (not counting fiber) at only 100 grams, or 25% of my calorie intake, but that's completely optional.

So here are my quick and dirty carb tracking rules. Feel free to add any conditions you like, but this basic plan gives you maximum flexibility with your diet without sacrificing weight loss results:

➢ Limit the high-glycemic index foods. Those with an index score of 70 or more. This mainly means save potatoes, white bread and short-grained rice for special occasions and don't include them in your regular diet. I'll cover specific techniques to swap these ingredients with tasty and carb free alternatives in the recipe section. Don't stress over the low scoring carbs under 70 on the index, at least after you've made significant weight loss progress. The bottom line is, if you're staying away from those big carb bombs and strictly controlling your sugar intake, it's quite difficult to exceed your total carb allowance no matter what you eat.

➢ Subtract sugar from your total carbs, not separately. You can count sugar alcohols at only half the gram rate as regular sugar though.

➢ If you're following a low-carb diet, subtract the carbs from dietary fiber, since those are not readily digestible. Otherwise, you're making it harder to follow that diet and thus more likely to slip up. For example, if you're fretting over the carbs in healthy natural foods like fruits, vegetables, nuts, beans and whole grains, once you subtract the fiber you'll see you haven't come close to busting your carb budget yet. In fact, go out of your way to get more fiber in your diet than you're used to. Constipation is a common side effect of going sugar free, especially in the early weeks.

That's it. Feel free to define your own carb intake rules, but if you're following these minimum steps, you can't go wrong.

4) You can keep eating all the normal meals you enjoy (except junk food), as long as you replace a few simple ingredients.

This is the key to lasting success. Most people trying to follow a Keto diet get burned out in a hurry, what with the giant list of no-no foods and rather bland tasting list of safe foods. But with a few easy tweaks, you can replace all the unhealthy sugars and unneeded carbs in any recipe with sugar-free and low to zero carb alternatives. This book will show you not just how to replace these ingredients, but do so in a way that leaves the end result tasting and looking nearly identical to the original recipe. If not better!

That's it. Don't sweat the details. If you're following these broad rules, you will lose weight fast and keep it off, while exponentially reducing your risk of all sorts of health complications. Best of all, you'll be happier, more confident and less stressed than you've ever been on a diet.

Everything else are just minor details once you've implemented these tight sugar controls. At least within the specific context of weight control. Exercise more (hopefully you do) or don't. Follow any specific diet regime you prefer. Whatever. That stuff is important for your overall health, but not so much for controlling your weight if you're already cutting out sugar and starchy carbs.

That's because the positive effects of these other programs are minor in comparison to the game changing benefits from turning off the sugar valve. For example, burning an extra 500 or so calories working out every week is great, or trimming down another 500 calories from your weekly diet by eating lower fat foods is also outstanding. But this is still small potatoes compared to the 7,000-14,000 calories you've already cut out of your weekly intake with your sugar-free diet. Remember, long term success is all about staying flexible.

Now, don't take this to mean that it's a waste of time to exercise daily. I wish I had appreciated all the benefits of even a light workout regime. For one small example, exercise would have kept me from getting so much loose skin after my sudden weight loss, but that's a subject for another book.

Safety note: If you're like most of my clients, you were probably referred to this book by your doctor. If you have not done so already, mention to your physician that you're planning to adopt a Ketonic diet. This is especially important if you're taking any sort of medication, have any type of diabetes or have high blood pressure. Keto is usually perfectly safe for those conditions, but there is a good chance your doctor will need to adjust the doses of your medications.

As difficult as it is to truly cut out all that hidden sugar from your diet, the good news is that once you've done so the hard work is over. When you're really sticking to that 25 gram a day sugar limit, everything else in your diet is quite flexible.

You can add on any other diet plan you please to this new lifestyle. Go vegan, go low-carb, go high-protein, Paleo, dairy-free, nut-free—whatever you want. Once you're gone with the sugar, or at least strictly capping your sugar intake, you will be on a sustainable route to hit your weight and health goals no matter what other dietary changes you make.

What's The Big Deal About Sugar?

First, I want to clear up some common misconceptions about sugar, some of which I believed myself for too long. To prove I'm not some sort of militant anti-sugar fanatic (wink wink at certain friends and family!), let's clarify a few of the biggest false negative claims about sugar:

1) There is NO evidence that sugar directly causes cancer or accelerates its growth.

According to the Mayo Clinic,[7] a far more reliable source of information than health "gurus" trying to sell you some diet plan, there is no direct link between sugar consumption and an increased risk of any form of cancer.

In multiple animal and human experiments, feeding extra sugar into cancerous cells had no effect on cancer growth, while depriving cancer cells of sugar also had no change on the rate of spread. These are the official findings by the US FDA, American Institute for Cancer Research[8] and the United Kingdom's National Health System[9].

With that said, excessive sugar intake is by far the most common risk factor in the obesity epidemic, which *is* linked to higher cancer risks. Not to mention diabetes, heart disease, and, well, practically every non-communicable disease out there. The CDC considers obesity the number 1 epidemic in the US and entire Western world for good reason—it's killing us faster than opiates, alcohol, terrorists and texting while driving combined! Just about tied with tobacco use. Granted, there's nothing about sugar itself that is making us fat, but rather the endless tide of hidden sugar in our food supply that's causing us to consume far more calories than we need.

2) Sugar is NOT X times more addictive than cocaine or other drugs.[10]

This was the hardest for me to believe at first, since there are some popular doctors and one interesting study on animals arguing otherwise. However, the bulk of the medical

---

[7] Mayo Clinic. (November 3, 2018) *Cancer Causes: Popular Myths About The Causes Of Cancer.* *H*ttps://www.mayoclinic.org/diseases-conditions/cancer/in-depth/cancer-causes/art-20044714

[8] American Institute for Cancer Research. *Sugar and cancer risk.* *H*ttp://www.aicr.org/reduce-your-cancer-risk/diet/sugar-and-cancer-risk.html

[9] Brighton and Sussex University Hospitals NHS Trust. (July, 2017). *Facts About Sugar And Cancer.* *H*ttps://www.bsuh.nhs.uk/wp-content/uploads/sites/5/2016/09/Facts-about-sugar-and-cancer.pdf

[10] Westwater, M. L., Fletcher, P., Ziauddeen, H. (November, 2016). *Sugar addiction: the state of the science.* European Journal of Nutrition. Vol. 55, p. 55. Https://link.springer.com/article/10.1007/s00394-016-1229-6

community overwhelmingly "fails to accept the null hypothesis" that sugar is more addictive than opiates.[11]

The confusion seems to come down to semantics. While added sugar is absolutely habit-forming and hard to quit because it creates a psychological dependency in your brain, that's not the same clinical definition of a chemical addiction. This addiction is nowhere on par with opiates or other "hard" drugs. So yes, there are some withdrawal symptoms, and sometimes they are intense, but we're not talking about an elaborate rehab process. You don't need any special help nor Herculean willpower to live free of sugar.

You just need the desire to change your life before sugar takes your life.

3) You don't have to give up all sugar to live sugar-free, just all ADDED sugar.

I'm not talking out of both sides of my mouth. Or at least not trying to! I'm just pointing out the nuance that tends to get lost in all the unnecessarily complicated health information online: you can still lose weight and get healthy fast even if you take in some sugar. Cutting out all sugar and forcing your body to burn fat instead of glucose for energy is just the fastest way to reach your goals. Once you've hit your target weight, then simply stick to natural sugars and avoid added ones to stay there.

There are no special chemical properties of sugar that make it hazardous to your health. What makes sugar unhealthy is taking in more than you need, which your body stores as fat for a rainy day. Now, this was a great survival trait in the prehistoric days, but we're not hunters and gatherers anymore. Sugar is no longer a rare treat we can only indulge in after a lucky foraging expedition. Sugar is now pumped artificially into most of our food supply and you have to go out of your way to only consume the recommended amount. That's why it's so important to eliminate the added sugars in your diet. On the plus side, since you can treat all these sugars the same, it's a lot easier to keep track of your sugar intake if you know what you're looking for.

For example, sugar alone doesn't even directly cause tooth decay.[12] However, adding more than the recommended amounts of sugar to your diet feeds the bacteria in your mouth, causing them to secrete more acid than normal, which breaks down the tooth enamel and so on. In short, sugar itself isn't the problem. It's how much we're taking in that's killing us.

After all, every cell in your body needs some glucose (sugar) from your bloodstream for fuel. We get that blood sugar from every type of food containing carbohydrates,

11 US News & World Report. (November 16, 2018). *Health Pros Call BS on Sugar Addiction.* *H*ttps://health.usnews.com/wellness/food/articles/2018-11-16/sugar-is-addictive-bs-these-health-pros-say

[12] O'Connor, Anahad. (August 16, 2010). "The Claim: More Sugar Leads to More Cavities." *The New York Times. H*ttps://www.nytimes.com/2010/08/17/health/17real.html

including vegetables, fruits, whole grains and low-fat dairy sources. Some glucose is even produced within our bodies from protein.

But it's the simple sugars that are added in food processing that are making us fat. If you're not carefully reading those nutrition labels, you're taking in exponentially more calories than you need. And your body has been conditioned by millennia of survival obsessed evolution to be a hoarder. It won't waste anything and instead turns every extra calorie into fat, then stuffs these unneeded energy stores in every nook and cranny it can find in your body.

But again, it's not even fat alone that's the real danger. The root cause of all of this is that we're adding way too much sugar into our diets and doing so secretly, which is leading to all sorts of indirect health consequences.

How Much Total Sugar Do You Need?

To put the problem in perspective, the absolute maximum amount of natural and added sugar you should take in is 10% of your total caloric intake per day. With 5% being the recommended level. [13] And this is from both natural sugar and added sugar sources. So, if you're following a normal recommended diet, you can't consume more sugar every day than:

- 38 grams for men
- 25 grams for women
- 20 grams for children under 12 years old
- 32 grams for children between 12-18 years old
  Note: recommended sugar levels for children are much more flexible and can vary by plus/minus 50% from these guidelines depending on age, metabolism, growth spurts and physical activity levels.

Now remember: these guidelines assume you're an average person, in terms of weight and activity levels, and in good health. So if you're already overweight, then that 5% sugar budget is way too much. Your natural and added sugar calorie level needs to be as close to zero as possible to see significant weight loss.

Sounds simple enough, yet the average American gulps down a whopping 126 grams of processed sugar a day.[14] That number is surely an underestimate, since it's calculated by simply dividing the estimated cane sugar and fructose syrup sales from major corporations in America by the nation's total population. It doesn't take into account smaller sugar

---

[13] World Health Organization. (2015). *Sugars Intake For Adults And Children.*
https://www.who.int/nutrition/publications/guidelines/sugars_intake/en/
[14] The Diabetes Council. (July 10, 2018). *45 Alarming Statistics on American's Sugar Consumption and the Effects of Sugar on Americans' Health.*
https://www.thediabetescouncil.com/45-alarming-statistics-on-americans-sugar-consumption-and-the-effects-of-sugar-on-americans-health/

pushers or natural forms of sugar like fruit juice. And it sure as heck doesn't consider the unique lifestyles of people addicted to sugar.

In my experience coaching ex-sugar addicts (including myself), once we audit sugar intake together, the real-world number of daily calories coming from sugar in all its forms is usually between 30-40% of our total energy consumption. Even worse, we aren't exactly sticking to the recommended 2,000 daily calorie limit for women, or 2,500 for men. Not even close, thanks to the addictive deliciousness of all this sugary crap.

Let's face it, most of us sugar addicts are wolfing down 3,000+ calories on any given day. Which means more than *1,000* extra calories worth of pure energy that you don't need and will never use is getting sucked up by your body as fat.

Every… single… day!

This is where a lot of folks just shrug and say something like: "Oh, don't be so dramatic. I'll go for a walk after dinner and take the stairs instead of the elevator at work. If I get some more exercise, it'll all balance out in the end."

Technically that's true but take a second to check any calorie burner calculator. Depending on your weight and heart rate, you're going to need between 90-180 minutes of continuous high-intensity cardio exercise to burn off 1,000 extra calories.[15] By high intensity I don't mean fast-walking or jogging, but rather full-speed sprinting for 1.5 to 3 hours. Bear in mind, that's just to *maintain* your current weight with this sugarlicious diet. You wouldn't actually lose any weight with this Herculean workout schedule; just keep from gaining more. And you would need to do this crazy workout every day without a single rest day. Not even Olympic athletes could keep that extreme exercise regime going for long.

And that's just the tip of the iceberg, since most of these sugars are added to already high-fat or nutrient-poor processed foods, which add even more empty calories that are also converted into extra glucose

This is even worse for kids under the age of 18, where almost 40% of their total daily energy consumption is in the form of empty calories from added sugar.[16]

Half of those empty calories came from just six kinds of foods:

---

[15] WebMD. *Exercise Calorie Burning Calculator.* Https://www.webmd.com/fitness-exercise/healthtool-exercise-calculator

[16] Reedy, J., Krebs-Smith, SM. (2010). *Dietary Sources Of Energy, Solid Fats, And Added Sugars Among Children And Adolescents In The United States.* Https://www.ncbi.nlm.nih.gov/pubmed/20869486

- Soda
- Fruit drinks
- Dairy desserts
- Grain desserts (cookies, doughnuts, etc.)
- Pizza
- Whole milk

Note on Artificial Sweeteners

Here's where things get controversial when I'm coaching folks on this new lifestyle. I want to clear the air quickly so we don't get bogged down in technical minutia and miss out on the big picture. While personally I avoid artificial sweeteners and stick to all-natural sugar substitutes, like organic stevia or birch xylitol, that's merely my opinion. I have no reliable studies nor statistics proving that all those laboratory concocted chemicals are unsafe or lead to other complications, such as increased cravings for sugar. I just prefer to be on the cautious side. I try to follow the old adage: "If it's a plant, it's food; if it was made in a plant, it's not for you." Still, you'll have to decide for yourself.

With that said, most artificial sweeteners have no calories in them. They're also not carbohydrates, so they won't have any direct effect on your blood sugar level. Now, there is some compelling but not yet conclusive evidence that consuming large amounts of high-intensity artificial sweeteners can interfere with the insulin levels in your body, so play it safe and take these chemicals in moderation.[17]

Nonetheless, from the strictly narrow point of view of only cutting sugar from your diet, artificial sweeteners are an effective tool that provides the sweetness you're craving without the weight gain, indirect negative health effects or habit-forming properties found in sugar. This is the FDA's official stance,[18] and I (grudgingly) admit I can't prove them wrong. I'm going to take a quick break before I bite my tongue all the way off…

Ok, so, the decision whether to consume artificial sweeteners is a personal lifestyle choice that should not distract you from the big picture health benefits of cutting sugar from your diet. At a minimum though, please only ingest those high-intensity artificial sweeteners that have been approved by the FDA. Which, as of this writing, includes just the following:[19]

---

[17] Harvard School of Public Health. (2018). *Low Calorie Sweeteners*.
Https://www.hsph.harvard.edu/nutritionsource/healthy-drinks/artificial-sweeteners/

[18] US Food and Drug Administration. (August 2, 2018). *Additional Information about High-Intensity Sweeteners Permitted for Use in Food in the United States*.
Https://www.fda.gov/food/ingredientspackaginglabeling/foodadditivesingredients/ucm397725.htm

[19] American Diabetes Association. (December, 2014). *Low-Calorie Sweeteners*.
Http://www.diabetes.org/food-and-fitness/food/what-can-i-eat/understanding-carbohydrates/artificial-sweeteners/

Artificial Sweetener	Common Brand Names
Acesulfame potassium (Ace-K)	Sunett®, Sweet One®
Advantame	No registered brands yet
Aspartame	Equal®, NutraSweet®, Sugar Twin®
Luo Han Guo fruit extracts	Monk Fruit or SGFE
Neotame	Newtame®
Saccharin	Sweet'N Low®, Sweet Twin®, Necta Sweet®
Steviol glycosides	Truvia®, PureVia®, Stevia or Bertoni extract
Sucralose	Splenda®

How To Cut Through The Fog And Find What's Important In Those Nutrition Labels.

Everything on the front of a package is marketing hype that can't be trusted. Everything from the product's healthy sounding name, to the unverified health claims and the vaguely comforting color schemes are designed to trick you. Food manufacturers employ armies of marketing experts to better deceive consumers and get a slight edge over their competition. Nothing is going to change that business model, so we need to adapt. That means always, always and always read the nutrition label and list of ingredients on the back of every single product.

Doesn't matter if you're in a rush and the kids are screaming. If you just snag something with a green color scheme on the box and a bunch of nonsense claims about being "low sugar" and "all natural," then you're getting ripped off. Both in terms of price and getting hosed down with added processed sugars.

But it doesn't have to take long to save your life. Seconds, really. Unless you're following some other specific diet plan, all you need to worry about is added sugar and total carbs. I'm not suggesting you completely ignore fat, but that's a separate issue. For our purposes, we only need to check three things to stay on track with our health goals:

1) Scan the ingredients list for those sneaky sources of hidden added sugars.

If you're trying to lose weight, then avoid added sugars like the plague. If you're already at a healthy weight, then you can enjoy your 25 to 38 grams of sugar daily, but no more or else you'll soon be right back where you started.

Remember, anything called a syrup or ending in -ose is a sugar. There are so many sneaky ways a company can pack sugar into their products, but the total carbs don't lie. If the package claims to be low sugar yet the total carbohydrate count is high, they've added a bunch of sugar.

2) Make sure you're not going to blow your entire daily sugar budget with a realistic serving of this single item.

While it helps, you don't have to plan out your meals before going to the store. Just making sure no single item is going to blow your sugar budget is enough to keep you on track, no matter what you do with the food later.

Note: by realistic servings I mean how much you know you're going to eat/drink at a time, which is rarely the same as the suggested serving size. For example, if the cereal's serving size says "1/2 cup," but you know darn well you're going to fill your breakfast bowl mostly full, then a realistic serving size for you is a full cup. Perhaps even a bit more.

It might not be possible to do the math in your head on the spot, but you can guesstimate how much you'll use on average from your past use of this or similar products. For example, one bag of whatever might say it includes 20 servings, but you know from experience that you can only dip into the bag five times before it's empty. In this case, simply divide the total sugar and carbs in the package by five to see if it really fits in your diet. Maybe your actual servings will be a bit smaller or larger, but they'll average out to this number.

3) Make sure the net carbs, including sugar/sugar alcohols but minus dietary fiber, are not unreasonably high.

If you're following a low-carb diet, you'll want to track net carbs as closely as sugar. Even if you're not on a low-carb diet, you still need to limit high-carb foods or you'll blow right past the healthy levels of carbohydrates in short order. And remember, since carbs are eventually broken down into sugar, then what's the point of getting rid of the added sugars if you're just going to replace them with an overdose of natural carbs?

If you don't want to do the math, you can stay away from high carb foods with two simple rules of thumb:

Avoid anything with a glycemic index score over 70 or if the calories from total (minus fiber) carbs is more than 20% of the DV (Daily recommended value for a 2,000-calorie diet).

This all might seem like no-brainer common sense. Read the nutrition label and keep track of how many sugars and carbs you're taking in. So what's all the fuss about?

Well, the biggest problem is the vast sea of hidden sugar flooding our food supply. Before the processed food craze that began in the 1950's, staying away from sugar was pretty straightforward—don't drink too much soda or eat sweet treats. Quite simple.

Unfortunately, things are far more complicated nowadays. First, the sugar industry has adopted Big Tobacco's lobbying and misinformation tactics. While that's a topic for a whole other book, remember when Coca Cola was the top sponsor of the Academy of Pediatrics' healthychildren.org site? They donated over $3 million.[20] Which was only part of a broader campaign to peg all the well-documented weight and health issues of excessive sugar consumption on simply not exercising enough, rather than having anything to do with your diet.

But that's just the tip of the iceberg.

One of the sneakiest tricks that food manufacturers employ nowadays is just breaking up the sources of sugar to be less conspicuous. So instead of adding 100 grams of cane sugar to an item, they'll add 10 grams of corn sweetener, and another 10 from glucose, plus the same amount in dextrin, dextrose, maltose, etc... Still 100 grams of total added, processed sugar in the box, but it's now divvied up 10 ways.

---

[20] PBS NewsHour. (Sep 30, 2015). *American Academy Of Pediatrics Decides Relationship With Coke Is Not So Sweet.* Https://www.pbs.org/newshour/show/coke

This minor trick is quite clever. A quick glance at the ingredients doesn't show anything explicitly labeled as sugar. Even a savvy shopper who recognizes that those -ose terms are all disguised sugars might not consider them a big deal. Afterall, the faux sugars are way down on the bottom of the ingredient list. And the box does say "low sugar."

But remember that "low sugar" is a marketing buzzword with no FDA standard definition. Once you add all those "trace elements" of sugar up, you'll usually see that a single serving will bust your sugar budget.

Sugar Disguises

This is not some theoretical possibility though. There are actually 61 different types of sugars approved by the FDA! Some don't even have to be labeled as added sugar. Lowering the weights of each type of sugar to force the ingredients lower on the label is common industry practice. Especially for items marketed to children. In fact, 74% of packaged foods, including all sorts of supposedly "healthy" products have more than one added sugar.[21]

At the moment, the current list of sugars available in the US for food companies to play around with are:

			Powdered
Agave nectar	Corn sweetener	Golden syrup	sugar
Barbados sugar	Corn syrup	Grape sugar	Raw sugar
		HFCS (high-fructose	
Barley malt	Corn syrup solids	corn syrup)	Refiner's syrup
Barley malt syrup	Date sugar	Honey	Rice syrup
	Dehydrated cane		
Beet sugar	juice	Icing sugar	Saccharose
Brown sugar	Demerara sugar	Invert sugar	Sorghum syrup
Buttered syrup	Dextrin	Malt syrup	Sucrose
			Sugar
Cane juice	Dextrose	Maltodextrin	(granulated)
Cane juice	Evaporated cane		
crystals	juice	Maltol	Sweet sorghum
	Free-flowing brown		
Cane sugar	sugars	Maltose	Syrup
Caramel	Fructose	Mannose	Treacle
			Turbinado
Carob syrup	Fruit juice	Maple syrup	sugar
	Fruit juice		
Castor sugar	concentrate	Molasses	Yellow sugar
Coconut palm			Powdered
sugar	Glucose	Muscovado	sugar
Coconut sugar	Glucose solids	Palm sugar	Raw sugar
Confectioner's			
sugar	Golden sugar	Panocha	Refiner's syrup

Some of these are particularly sneaky, since they can be labeled as general carbohydrates rather than added sugar. Maltodextrin is one of the most common offenders. While legally not required to be listed as added sugar on the nutrition label, maltodextrin

---

[21] Ng, S.W., Slining, M.M., & Popkin, B.M. (2012). "Use of caloric and noncaloric sweeteners in US consumer packaged foods, 2005-2009." *Journal of the Academy of Nutrition and Dietetics*, 112(11). Http://sugarscience.ucsf.edu/hidden-in-plain-sight/#.XGVBclxKiUk

has a whopping 105 score on the glycemic index! In comparison, plain old table sugar scores only 64.

If you take nothing else from this book, simply carrying a copy of this sugar ID list with you everywhere you go and not eating or buying anything with more than two matches will go a long way to controlling your sugar levels and bringing down your weight.

Remember, manufacturers only have to list total sugar in their products and not clarify what's been added. Still, there are four quick ways to tell if they've added sugar to a package, even if you don't have this list handy.

1. If any of the ingredients end in "-ose," such as maltose, dextrose, fructose, glucose, lactose, or sucrose, then it's almost guaranteed they were added in processing.

2. Same goes for any type of syrup, such as fructose, molasses or corn syrup.

3. Natural sweeteners. While there's nothing wrong with these in principle, if the company is mentioning any type of natural sweetener, that's just a pleasant way to declare they added a bunch of sugar. It doesn't matter what form the sweetener takes, such as corn, honey or fruit juice concentrates; they're still talking about unnaturally elevated levels of sugar.

4. Fruit juice concentrate. Don't be tempted to shrug and say, "Oh, that's just fruit. No big deal." Yes, fruit is all-natural and the concentrate still contains vitamins, but we're also talking about 3-7 times the natural sugar content. And your body will treat that concentrated fruit juice the same as high fructose corn syrup and start stockpiling it in your fat reserves.

Flavor Blends Listed As A Top Three Ingredient

This is one of the most nefarious tricks out there, but thankfully one of the easiest to spot. An increasingly common practice among food manufacturers, especially those hocking "all natural" and "organic" foods, is to just bundle their sugar and other chemicals into some form of seasoning blend. Then they'll add a token amount of fruit or something healthy and give the new concoction some pleasing, friendly name. Whatever they call it, the blend is little more than a pile of sugar sporting a pretty new dress.

Usually, this blend is trademarked, so that helps to spot the subterfuge fast. What really stands out though is how a spice, blend or seasoning agent is in the first few items on the ingredient list. If it's just a flavoring ingredient, then why the heck does it make up so much of the mass? Nine times out of ten, the answer is simply because you're looking at a sugar bomb. Take a quick peek at the total carb amount. If you see few to no sugars, only a bit of fiber but +20% of the daily recommended amount of carbohydrates per serving… yeah, that's a sugar booby trap. So stay clear.

Package Labeling Tricks

Hand in hand with the ingredient list shenanigans, there are so many labeling tricks food manufacturers can use to stuff extra sugar in your food without your knowledge. I'm not saying to give into the paranoia and go vegan (there's added sugar in many types of vegetables even!), but stay skeptical of all those meaningless and unregulated marketing terms like:

- **Non-GMO, USDA Organic or All Natural**. None of these ambiguous terms prove anything about the health value of the food, let alone if it's really sugar-free or even low-sugar.
- **Low Sugar**. This has no standard definition and can mean whatever the manufacturer wants.
- **No Refined Sugars**. This just means no extra white table sugar was added. It doesn't keep them from loading the product down with fruit concentrates or other high calorie sweeteners that have an even higher glycemic score than simple sucrose.

Now, some food claims are regulated by the FDA, [22] but with loopholes so wide you could drive a truck full of lobbyists through them. You can also replace "sugar" with "carbs" or "fat" in the following claims to see the same tricks at work.

- **No Calories, Zero Calories, Calorie Free**. This all seems like a no-brainer, since if there aren't any calories inside, there can't be any sugar, right? The devil is in the details though. To make these claims, the product doesn't need to have zero calories. Just less than five calories per serving, and those serving sizes tend to be ultra-small. Worse, those calories can, and often do, come from just sugar so the product tastes good and keeps folks coming back. Remember: five calories equal 1.25 grams of sugar, and with a budget of 25 grams per day for a woman, those "zero calorie" snacks are taking a giant, stealthy chunk out of your sugar budget with every bite.

- **Reduced Sugar or Less Sugar**. This simply means there's 25% less sugar per serving compared to the original item. An easy way around this is to pump up the sugar content of the older, and usually now discontinued item, so there's no significant change in the new product's sugar content.

- **No Added Sugars or Without Added Sugars**. All this means is they haven't *added* any sugar in the processing, so stay skeptical and carefully read the nutrition label. By this standard, a 5-pound bag of raw cane sugar could technically be labeled as "No Added Sugar."

---

[22] American Heart Association. (March, 2017). *Food Packaging Claims.* Https://www.heart.org/en/healthy-living/healthy-eating/eat-smart/nutrition-basics/food-packaging-claims

Another fun loophole is that manufacturers can skirt the no sugar added claim by using sugar alcohols. Yes, sugar alcohol contains only half the calories as sugar carbs, but that's still a considerable hidden source of added sugar.

- **Sugar Free, Zero Sugar, No Sugar, Without Sugar, Trivial Source of Sugar, Negligible Source of Sugar, Dietarily Insignificant Source of Sugar.**

These are my favorite claims, because they seem so clear-cut but are the most misleading. They can make this claim as long as there is less than 0.5 grams of sugar per serving. How big is a serving? 100 grams, 10 grams? There's a lot of wiggle room here.

In addition, once you look at the ingredient list, you'll see "sugar free" is almost always code for "we've loaded this with lower calorie sugar substitutes." Sometimes that's a good thing, in the case of natural extracts with no calories like monk fruit, but quite often they're using sugar alcohol or other sweeteners that are low sugar, but not completely sugar free. So again, always carefully read the ingredients. Even if you still want to consume these items, you'll need to budget accordingly to make sure you're not going over your daily sugar limit.

Common Sources of Hidden Sugar

A regular complaint I hear from recovering sugar addicts is: "I haven't touched a soda, candy bar or anything like that in months, but I've only lost a few pounds. I thought this program was supposed to work faster?"

First, my hat's off to anyone who can take the plunge and has already cut out so much sugar from their diet... but the obvious stuff like brand name sugar water and junk food isn't where all the added sugar comes from. Much of it, yes, but "free" sugar is free range and wandering around everywhere. Worse, when most people cut out the junk food, they tend to satisfy their sugar cravings, albeit unknowingly, by indulging in more traditional foods that are loaded down with hidden sugar and empty complex carbohydrates.

So if you're following a Keto-like diet and not seeing major results, here are the most likely sources of added sugar gumming up the works. You'll notice that most come from otherwise healthy foods. This doesn't mean you have to avoid these things at all costs, but if anything in your shopping cart matches this list, you should pay extra attention to the ingredient list and nutrition label.

- **Anything labeled as "low fat or fat-free."** In theory, fats should have nothing to do with sugar and carbs. However, the simple reality is that everyone wants low fat food, but they want it to taste as good as the full fat version. Food manufacturers are happy to oblige by shoving in all sorts of fat-free flavor enhancers, all based on some form of super sweet carbohydrate. In other words, these are sugar landmines you need to handle with care.

  You'll see this quite often in flavored yogurts. While nutritious, most low-fat yogurts are heavily sweetened with sugar, fruit or honey. So read the labels carefully. It's usually better to choose full-fat, natural or unflavored Greek yogurt. You can toss in your own berries or non-sugar sweeteners when you get home. The marginal increase in fat you're consuming is nothing compared to all the sugar you're not taking in.

- **Anything "enhanced" or "fortified."** This is most often seen in beverages, especially vitamin water and sports drinks. Even if the label claims to be sugar free, these are common places to use non-sugar sugars, like maltodextrin. The red flag will be your "water" is somehow packed with carbohydrates. So read those labels with care.

- **Anything marketed towards a certain diet.** "Low + anything." Remember, when something is taken out of a processed food item, something else must be added to keep things tasty. In most cases, sugar fits their needs. A few extra grams per serving could bust your sugar allowance on a single diet item, even if the product still is low carb, low fat, low sodium or high protein or high fiber.

- **Instant everything.** Even otherwise healthy things, like oatmeal, will usually have several extra teaspoons of sugar. Try to stick to the plain old varieties. Plus, you can microwave just about anything, even if it takes an extra minute or you need to add some water first. So why pay more for the convenience anyway?

- **Bread**. It should go without saying that anything processed or even pre-sliced is likely to be loaded with added sugar. Now, I get it. Fresh bread from a bakery can get expensive, especially if you have a large family. It also doesn't last as long, since it's not full of sugar preservatives. And who has time to bake their own bread out of alternative flours? Every now and again, sure, but every single day? Not sustainable. So at the very least, stick to whole-grain bread, which usually has less than half the sugars of white bread.

- **Breakfast cereal.** I'm not talking about the obvious diabetes bombs marketed to children, which are little more than whole sugar cubes dusted with some corn flakes for decoration. Even many "healthy" adult-oriented cold cereals are loaded down with more sugar per serving than soda. Underneath all those misleading labels about being "high fiber" or "Fortified with vitamins A-Z," you'll find the average adult cereal contains 18% sugar by weight.[23] In comparison, normal Coca Cola contains "only" 9% sugar by weight.

  To be fair, many of these are natural sugar sources that contain plenty of vitamins and minerals, rather than just empty calories like with table sugar. Nonetheless, you need to read the label to recognize how much sugar you're taking in and budget accordingly.

- **Canned fruits and vegetables.** Since sugar is both a flavor enhancer and cheap preservative, so many brands add significant extra sugar to what would otherwise be a perfectly healthy choice. So double check the added sugar list on the label.

- **Granola.** Again, this is one of those perfectly healthy foods that's ruined by all the added sugar. Generally the added sugar comes from concentrated honey or other natural sweeteners rather than table sugar, so pay attention to the nutrition label and not the fancy packaging. If you're really craving something crunchy, a good compromise is to use granola crumbles as a topping for something else instead of a standalone snack.

- **Dried fruit, whether as a snack or flavor topping.** Fresh fruit isn't usually a big source of hidden sugar. However, when the fruit is dried out and then repackaged, that sugar fructose becomes concentrated and packs many more calories per serving. So

---

[23] Environmental Working Group. (May, 2014). *Children's Cereals: Cereals Contain Far More Sugar Than Experts Recommend. H*ttps://www.ewg.org/research/childrens-cereals-sugar-pound/cereals-contain-far-more-sugar-experts-recommend

make sure you check the nutrition label and count the sugar grams and not just carbs here.

- **Pasta sauces, marinades, condiments and dressings.** These are the easiest to overlook, because sauces are usually just a little coup de grace for the larger meal. But don't underestimate the hidden sugar power here. For example, most brands of ketchup are made up of 22% sugar by weight. Even "fat-free" ranch dressing clocks in at 5% sugar. Make sure this is really where you want to spend your sugar budget.

- **"No added sugar" fruit juice or smoothies.** Yes, these are all-natural and great sources of vitamins and minerals, but that fruit concentrate is still packed with sugar. More so than even soda. Despite being vastly healthier for you, just a glass or two of pure fruit juice will bust your daily sugar budget. Instead of drinking concentrated juice, just eat the real fruit. You get the same taste as well as plenty of vitamins and fiber, but with a fraction of the sugar. If you must have some juice, keep it in moderation and count it against your sugar budget. You can also always just water the juice down, half and half with sparkling water.

Cigarettes

Many smokers are afraid to quit tobacco as well at the same time they start any new diet plan, since nicotine does help suppress your appetite. This supposed help comes at an insane price to your life expectancy, but there are three more immediate reasons why it's a mistake to keep smoking while trying to slash sugar from your diet:

1) Cigarettes contain a significant amount of sugar. To smooth the tobacco's harsh natural flavor and, of course, make the cancer sticks even more addictive, cigarette manufacturers load their products down with added sugars. In one study of 58 leading tobacco brands, each cigarette's average sugar content represented 17.4% of its weight.[24] That's gram for gram more sugar than you'll find in most sodas!

2) Don't fear the sudden weight gain that often comes from quitting tobacco cold turkey. That won't happen to you. This weight gain is caused by your brain searching for any substitute for the sudden nicotine embargo and, on a neurological level, sugar is the next best thing to nicotine. Stopping smoking doesn't start any magical chemical process in your body that increases weight gain. It's just those constant extreme cravings for anything sugary that tacks on the pounds. Since you'll already be switching to natural sugar substitutes, the weight gain won't follow. Not shouldn't, but *won't*.

---

[24] Jansen E, Cremers J, Borst S, Talhout R. (2014). "Simple Determination of Sugars in Cigarettes." *Journal of Analytical & Bioanalytical Techniques* 5:219. Https://www.omicsonline.org/open-access/simple-determination-of-sugars-in-cigarettes-2155-9872.1000219.php?aid=33331

3) If you're trying to get healthy, you're probably dreaming of quitting smoking someday. So why not hit two evil birds trying to kill you with the same rock-solid willpower? Afterall, you're going to suffer through nearly identical withdrawal symptoms with nicotine as with sugar, and for the same amount of time (3-7 days). So why go through this pain twice? It's not like the symptoms are cumulative. You won't get more stressed or more anxious by cutting out sugar and tobacco at the same time. The addiction withdrawal process is just as intense and lasts the same amount of time, whether you're abandoning one addiction or ten. Your mind will fight you in the same way and with the same intensity for a hit of dopamine, whether that fix is coming from sugar or nicotine. So take advantage of the opportunity and change your life!

Alcohol

With the obvious exception of sweetened cocktails and tonic water, most alcoholic beverages contain little to no sugar, but that doesn't mean there aren't massive indirect effects on your sugar intake from alcohol consumption. The situation is far more complicated than that. And you don't even need to be drunk to blow your sugar budget. Just a slight "buzz" is more than enough to throw your sugar-free lifestyle off track. You'll have to decide for yourself what is an appropriate amount and frequency to drink, but if you're planning on partying it up, you should definitely prepare by going sugar-free for a day or two beforehand to limit the damage.

First, many alcoholic drinks, especially but not exclusively beer, have a fairly high glycemic index. Meaning all those nutrition-empty carbs are just being turned into glucose and stored in your fat. So while not technically sugar, your body will treat it like a source of sugar. From a metabolic point of view, beer is basically liquid bread, which is why so many heavy drinkers joke about "drinking their dinner."

Second, even moderate amounts of alcohol slow down your body's metabolic process. The average person's liver can only process one "standard drink" worth of alcohol in an hour. So, if you drink more than one 12-ounce beer, or a 5-ounce glass of wine or a 1.5 ounce shot of liquor within an hour, your liver will be oversaturated and then it goes into panic mode.[25] In a last-ditch effort to expel this foreign "poison" from your body, you stop processing every other nutrient, including burning fat, until the alcohol is broken down to reasonable levels.

The net effect is that you feel hungry, but you're never quite full and satisfied no matter what you eat. Oh, and what is the go-to snack when you're out drinking? Anything sweet and salty. Or even better, something greasy, sugary and loaded with empty carbs, like you'll find in all the fast food joints that are open so late. Combine the limited food choices

---

[25] Mayo Clinic. (November, 2018). *Alcohol: Weighing Risks And Potential Benefits.* *H*ttps://www.mayoclinic.org/healthy-lifestyle/nutrition-and-healthy-eating/in-depth/alcohol/art-20044551

available when you're out on the town with your lower inhibitions, and, well... you're probably not going to make the smartest dietary decisions.

How Anyone Can Adopt This Lifestyle Regardless Of Budget Or Life Circumstances

Yeah, yeah. I've tried every fad diet out there. How's this going to be any different?

The difference between past diets and now is this is a lifestyle change. I am in it for the long haul. This can be a blessing or a curse, depending on your mindset.

On the one hand, you don't have to stick to some ultra-specific diet plan or grueling exercise regime for X days to see results. All you have to do is follow a fairly simple checklist to keep track of your sugar intake and, voila, the weight will fall off and your health will improve faster than ever. On the other hand, the changes you're making are permanent, so you need a whole new level of commitment. You can't just motivate yourself by saying, "Stay strong. All I have to do is tough it out for a few months…"

When I broke my sugar addiction, I didn't have the cravings. That made it easier for me to make the healthy choices. Your taste buds change. I can eat a blueberry now and it is equivalent to me eating that candy bar. I also lost weight so rapidly after my cold turkey split from sugar that I saw results immediately. Let me tell you that is a great motivator and more proof that sugar was my problem.

So any time I have a moment of weakness, I remember how bad it was before I broke my sugar addiction. I'll go back and read my notes or look at old photos and that is enough to keep me on the right track. This is a lifestyle change not a diet or a fad.

Come on! I'm just way too busy to cook healthy meals three times a day.

I hear you there. When I started this lifestyle, I was working eighty-hour weeks. Add in the commute time, family and household chores… most nights I bumped into myself going to bed. I barely had time to eat my junk food, let alone cook something healthy. But there's an easy fix.

Don't cook three times today. Cook once a day or cook one day a week or one day a month whatever it takes. My answer to I am way to busy is make time. My motto is what are you willing to give up in order to get what you need. And in this case you need to break your sugar addiction and live a healthier lifestyle. You may have to give up some of your busy time in order to get healthy.

You cannot afford to not make time for this. Inventory your day where can you shave off an hour or two. There has got to be something that you can give up in order to get what you need. There are so many easy healthy recipes out there. You can take one day a week and cook all your meals and freeze them. You can do semi homemade meals. They even sell healthy meals. Once you educate yourself on how to find the hidden sugars the rest is easy. You are worth the little investment to live sugar-free. Your life depends on it make time. Think about it, yes you have to give something up right now, but you will most definitely gain so much more in the end.

This sounds like a rich girl's diet. I work for a living. I can't afford to eat like this.

My response is you can't afford *not* to eat like this.

Sure, natural sugar substitutes are more expensive than table sugar. Fresh veggies and low carb noodles are always going to be pricier than a frozen pizza or box of Mac and Cheese. But the immediate sticker price of what you're putting in your body is only the tip of the iceberg. If you think spending $10-$50 more a month on food is too costly to change your diet, how are you going to handle the copays for all those inevitable insulin shots and preventable doctor visits? How can you put a price on adding years to your life?

This is a permanent lifestyle change. Not some popular summer diet. You can't just stick to this for a month, shave off a few pounds, pat yourself on the back and then go back to your old diet. You'll

I have changed my life and I have changed some bad habits that I had. It has taking me a year to realize that this is really a lifestyle change

I added up how much I was spending on junk food per day. I would have four large sweet teas from Dunkin' Donuts, and those are two dollars apiece. I would usually have Oreos or Doritos or Skittles or a Snickers bar per day. I added it up: $15 dollars a day in junk food. That was 420 dollars a month, in addition to my grocery bill. I'm no longer spending money on all that junk. My total food bill doesn't even reach $450 for the month. With the savings alone, I can afford the birch and almond flour and the healthy food choices. I think if you were to write down for a week what you spend you would see similar results. Remember my motto: what are you willing to give up in order to get what you need. I'm willing to give up the Dunkin' Donuts, Oreos, Doritos, skittles, Snickers in order to get healthy food.

How To Overcome Withdrawal Symptoms

With that said, there's no such thing as a free lunch. There is a short-term price to pay for changing your life in order to save your life.

If you've ever quit smoking, then you already know what I'm talking about. If you've never been addicted to tobacco, then the minute you cut your sugar intake you're going to sympathize with ex-smokers on a whole new level!

That's because, on the neurological level, there's not much of a difference between sugar and nicotine addiction. Both substances work the same way by constantly elevating the dopamine levels in the nucleus accumbens (NAc), and to roughly the same degree. In short, sugar, just like nicotine, rewires the mesolimbic reward pathway of the brain until you more than just crave it—your brain starts actively punishing you for not feeding its addiction until you cave in.

In fact, there's some evidence that common smoking cessation aides are just as effective at combating sugar withdrawal as tobacco dependency.[26] Though naturally, check with your doctor before trying anything like that.

Not that I'm trying to scare you. Thankfully, there are many natural substitutes for sugar that will make those cravings and withdrawal symptoms go away, whereas there's nothing a smoker can replace tobacco with.

Now, not everyone will go through all these symptoms. Plus, the length and severity of each symptom will differ based upon how much sugar you're used to consuming and a hundred other biological conditions.

Fatigue and Weakness

Likely the first and most noticeable symptom of sugar withdrawal is feeling spells of sluggishness, even fatigue as your blood sugar levels are adjusting. Both your brain and body are used to a certain level of sugar intake every day and you're suddenly flipping the script. Your body will adapt fast by just dipping into your ample fat reserves for more glucose. This all causes sudden drops in your blood sugar, and hence your "energy" levels, but don't worry. Your body is a self-regulating system that will sort itself out quite fast. The less added sugar you take in, the more fat you burn to compensate. And as your body mass shrinks and your metabolism improves, the less glucose your body needs to lug around all that weight.

---

[26] Shariff, M., Quik, M., et al. (March 30, 2016). *Neuronal Nicotinic Acetylcholine Receptor Modulators Reduce Sugar Intake.*
Https://journals.plos.org/plosone/article?id=10.1371/journal.pone.0150270

However, your brain is more stubborn. Once you cut out or even seriously cut down your sugar intake, your dopamine levels drop. In addition, the neurotransmitters that regulate pain perception, acetylcholine, will be more active and sensitive.[27] Thankfully, this passes quite fast, usually spiking in intensity within 24 hours and completely past after five days. Afterwards, you'll feel more energetic than ever before, with fewer up and down mood swings since your body will maintain a more "regular" and even blood sugar level.

How to overcome:

- Stay well hydrated.
- Breathing exercises and/or meditation
- Cold compresses
- Bed rest

Extreme Cravings

This is the classic "hangry" phase that so many people worry about. Everyone's cravings are expressed differently, but these symptoms go a bit further than the common discomfort as your body's blood sugar levels adjust. These are all caused by your desperate brain begging for its favorite dopamine release trigger. This phase is marked by not just longing for sugary delights, but often includes mood swings, momentary confusion and mild spells of lightheadedness. The cravings are triggered by a variety of physiological factors that are out of your control, so you can expect random periods of mild but temporary irritability and anxiousness no matter what you do.

In some extreme situations, especially if your sugar detox is coming on the heels of particularly stressful life events, you might even experience headaches or other physical ailments. While the last one is rare, you might even feel aches and pains that mimic fibromyalgia or other musculoskeletal conditions. The good news is that these are simply caused by an oversensitivity to pain in your neurotransmitters that's only temporary. Still, obviously, consult with your physician if you're at all concerned about any physical or physiological changes.

The key thing to remember is that nothing lasts forever. Some people don't report any extreme cravings after the first few hours and some need a week before the most intense urges fade. Personally, my hard-core cravings peaked at three days and passed completely after five. A small price to pay for adding years to my life and exponentially increasing my quality of life in the meantime. What are you willing to give up in order to get what you need?

---

[27] Avena, N., Rada, P., and Hoebel, G. (May, 2007). *Evidence For Sugar Addiction: Behavioral And Neurochemical Effects Of Intermittent, Excessive Sugar Intake.* *H*ttps://www.ncbi.nlm.nih.gov/pmc/articles/PMC2235907/

How to overcome:

- Stay busy, both physically and mentally. This is standard advice for quitting any type of addiction because it works so well, though it's the hardest to do because this step is usually accompanied by lethargy and fatigue. Still, if you push through, even moderate physical exercise releases other reward chemicals in your brain, like serotonin, endorphins and even dopamine.
- Stimulate your sweet tooth with natural alternative sweeteners, or even artificial sweeteners if that's all you have available.
- Try on your old clothes. I bought a great top and pants one size smaller than my current size so I had a physical manifestation of my goals in hand. This was a great way to keep me disciplined and focused on the future.
- Make sure you're using sugar-free toothpaste. Regular toothpaste is laced with sucrose, which will trigger cravings when it hits your tongue.
- If you slip up and just have to take a bite of something sugary, don't be afraid to chew and spit. I know I did. It may seem like a waste, but it's better than starting all over again and resetting the withdrawal symptom clock.
- Empty your home and car of all sugary items. This means even the small stuff, like breath mints, chewing gum, those sugar packets in your random stuff kitchen drawer, etc... You won't believe how desperate your mind can get for a sugar fix. Once you're come out of the withdrawal phase, then you can keep some sugar snacks around for the kids or guests, but don't risk it in the first two weeks.

Poor Sleep

Whether full blown insomnia or just interrupted REM periods that make you still feel drowsy when you wake up, poor sleep quality is a common side effect. Like all the other symptoms, it goes away on its own in short order. If you're still having trouble sleeping after a week, definitely see your doctor.

How to overcome:

- Avoid anything with caffeine in it after 1500.
- More physical exercise, even if it's just walking the dog more often.
- Allow yourself extra sleep time in the early stages of this program.
- Calming white noise background sounds
- A sleep mask
- Try some essential oil, such as lavender or peppermint scents.

Excessive Weight Loss

I hear your snort already. "Ha, I wish I had that problem!"

Once you radically alter your lifestyle, you'll see radical results. Your natural ketosis process will ramp up to overdrive and your body will loot your fat stores for energy at a mind-boggling rate. And sure, that's fabulous if you're just trying to slim your tummy down for beach season, but you're flirting with disaster if you keep up those extreme results for too long. Like everything in life, you need to strike a balance.

This is especially true if you're going 100% sugar free for any length of time. That means not just cutting out added sugars, but avoiding all fruits, dairy and starchy carbohydrates in general. You're depriving your body of external glucose, which means it needs to gut your, well, gut to survive. This is less of a diet and more of a quasi-starvation regime.

So after the heavy water-weight loss during the first two weeks, your fat burning rate should then be more consistent. Somewhere between 1-3 pounds a week. If you find yourself losing more than three pounds a week or you've already hit your original weight loss goal but are having trouble stopping, then you might be at risk for developing an eating disorder. Immediately consult with your doctor. This doesn't necessarily mean you need to quit what you're doing, but explain in detail your new diet and let the doctor show you various options to keep losing weight in safe and sustainable manner.

Negative reactions from your social network.

This really has nothing to do with your body, but dealing with emotional pushback from others is a part of the withdrawal process you will face. Some of your friends and maybe even family members won't react positively when they see you're eating differently. They might even openly mock you and say, "You're wasting your time." Or "It won't last. You'll give up soon." Or gossip that you must be "sick/depressed/have an eating disorder."

Well, c'est la vie. You can't control what anyone says, but you can put their criticism in context so it washes off your back. Remember, this is just their coping mechanism. They see you getting healthier and slimmer, but they're not ready to do what you have done. Your success is rubbing their failure in their face. So it's a natural response for them to try to tear you down rather than build themselves up. Always keep that in mind and you'll feel sympathy for them, rather than anger and sadness.

You might even have supposed friends that invite you out and try to trick you into eating sugar. Probably egg you on about being such an "unsocial picky eater."

Don't fall for it.

You're not too picky. Now that you're free of your addiction, you can eat anything you want. You've probably started eating and drinking healthy foods that you've never touched before, while they're the ones addicted to the same old sugar-filled junk food.

A fun way to show this without being too preachy is to make a game when you go out to dinner. When people ask me out, usually with a smirk on their face, I'll just smile and say, "Wherever you choose is fine." Then I'll dissect the menu like a detective, pulling up the menu ahead of time if I can and researching how much sugar is in everything. Once they see you ready to order before them, while spending your free time pointing out how much hidden sugar they don't know they're eating, most people will ease up.

Most, but not all. You will probably lose friends and begin avoiding even family members that continue to treat you this way. Realize they don't get it. They have not broken their sugar addiction. So just keep moving forward. Keep educating yourself and you might be able to help them one day.

Of course, the worst feedback you'll get is from yourself. Yes, you can go from morbidly obese to slim and healthy in a matter of months with this lifestyle... but don't expect your self-image to adapt so fast. Even though I lost 106 pounds, when I look in a mirror I sometimes don't see the small me. All I see is that 240 pound me. If you've lived your whole life under the scrutiny of our fat shaming culture, that's going to leave a mark on your psyche. But stay strong, because "this too shall pass."

You can take the fat out of a body quick, but you it requires years to take the fat mind out of the body. Being overweight leads to building up all sorts of insecurities, which fade so slowly. I said goodbye to the unhealthy sugar and vast amounts of fat 18 months ago, but it's still part of me. For example, I was always too embarrassed to be in photos, so I avoided them whenever possible. Even now I subconsciously flinch when someone whips out a camera and have to remind myself that I have nothing to be ashamed of.

Tips for Lasting Success

Hands-down the biggest complaint I hear when showing people how to adopt this lifestyle in practice is that "it's too expensive and time consuming." To be fair, I worried about the cost too, at first. I was living paycheck to paycheck at the time I started this program and all these "exotic" sugar and carb substitutes, such as almond flour and birch sweetener, seemed like unreasonable luxuries. Even purchasing fresh vegetables instead of the half-cost but sugar-filled canned variants was an extravagant waste.

Once I took the plunge though, those fears washed away. Just skipping my daily Dunkin' Donuts sweet tea or stopping the stress snacking on nutrient-empty potato chips and candies saved me more per day than I spent on these new ingredients in a week. Within a month, I was saving more money than ever before while actually spending less time in the kitchen. To say nothing of all the savings from not feeling sick all the time or racking up doctor's bills for easily preventable visits. You can do the same thing by following some simple steps:

1) *Trusting yourself is good, but control is better.*

A little bit of planning makes all the difference between success and failure with your sugar "detox." There are plenty of little things you can prepare for, but the key is to not trust blindly in your willpower, but rather control your urges ahead of time. You want to put up as many obstacles in the way of you and sugar as you can.

- Clear your home, car and workspace of anything sugary before you start. I don't just mean snacks, but everything with sugar in it. Including gum, loose sugar packets in the kitchen and even sugar-laden toothpaste. Replace everything with sugar-free versions beforehand.
- Plan out your meals ahead of time. Especially for those first 3-5 days. Aim for quick meals that you can prepare in minutes or even better, make the night before and put in the fridge. Your brain will make so many excuses to try and trick you into grabbing some fast food for breakfast or a pizza for dinner, or some candy on your break. But if it's easier to snag something healthy, you'll have the upper hand.
- Avoid parties, going out or high stress situations for those first few days. You want to be in control of the menu and eating schedule to avoid temptation. It's also a huge advantage if your sugar cravings are too intense to be able to withdraw and lie down until they pass.

2) *Stick to a food budget.*

The first and most important step you should take is to draft a food budget. I know, this was hard for me too. I'm still not great at it, but I'm getting better every month. Besides the obvious difficulty of accounting for a bunch of tiny expenses, especially if you have a large family, you're also auditing what and how much you eat. This can get embarrassing in a hurry and naturally, no one enjoys taking such a hard look at themselves.

Still, creating a food budget is worth the discomfort because this is the best way to guarantee lasting results. You'll be able to sustain your new lifestyle in perpetuity instead of busting your wallet and giving up after a month. Not to mention the powerful new confidence in yourself as you stay disciplined, plus more support from your partner or spouse when they see how dedicated you are to this new plan.

While there are many ways you can set up this budget, here are the keys to keep in mind:

- *Budget for the whole month, plan for the week, but surprise yourself every day.* This might not be exactly every month or week, but the general point is to set your food allowance budget based upon your pay cycle, your shopping list based upon how often you go to the store, but don't plan out every single meal ahead of time. Reward yourself with some variety every day.

- *Track what you're actually spending to update your estimates for next month.* This process is never really finished, since every month is a little bit different. However, if you're keeping every receipt and looking over them at the end of the month, you'll find yourself making ultra-precise estimates in a hurry. Plus, you'll be able to see what particular items you're spending the most on fast and be able to shop around for cheaper options, such as buying in bulk or online, to squeeze more out of your budget.

  This process doesn't need to take long. One thing that helps is to group all your personal food items on the grocery store conveyer belt by what's for you, what's for the rest of the family and what's a non-food item. Then you can pluck out and add up your expenses from many records in a matter of minutes. If you have really long shopping receipts, there are plenty of apps that scan a paper receipt and extract the information into Excel columns.

- *Prioritize and there'll never be more month left at the end of the money.*

  This is self-explanatory, but it's worth mentioning. If you're getting discouraged, sort your shopping list by must-haves and nice-to-haves. For example, fresh veggies are a must. Cheap meats like tuna, chicken and sausage are musts. Pricey things like good steaks, shrimp, etc are nice-to-haves. That way you'll always have a basic set of healthy, sugar free ingredients on hand no matter what happens to your budget.

3) *Always keep a healthy snack on hand.*

The best way to head off any surprise cravings or sudden drops in your blood sugar level is to have a sugar-free snack always available. Something a bit salty with high protein is usually enough to keep the worst sugar withdrawal symptoms at bay. I prefer mixed nuts or sorghum popcorn, but whatever you use, keep multiple stashes handy so you're never caught unprepared. That means a little snack pack in your car, your purse, your office, your gym bag—everywhere you go.

4) *Partner with someone*

If you're truly blessed, you'll have a good friend who's willing to take the no added sugar plunge with you. In that case, you're most of the way to success already.

Another thing would be to partner with someone else that is going to eat healthy and maybe do a co-op taking turns making the meals and splitting the cost on bulk buying items.

5) *Keep good notes in a journal.*

This doesn't have to be a full-blown diary, but more like an accounting ledger and tip sheet for yourself. Once you look up the carb and sugar count of something new, jot down a note to save you research time in the future. If you keep finding yourself desiring something in particular but can't eat it because it'll bust your sugar budget, then make a note to look up a sugar-free alternative recipe when you get a chance.

6) *Buy specialty ingredients in bulk.*

Besides the obvious fact that this is the cheapest way to buy some of these more expensive sugar and high carb substitutes, keeping a large stock of healthy ingredients on hand is a great way to make sure you actually use them. Convenience is the siren song of sugar, so head off the urge to order out by always having sugar-free materials for a quick snack or meal handy. And the cost savings can be huge, especially if you sign up with one of the many free websites that notify you about price drops on any item you're interested in on Amazon or other major retailers.

7) *Adjust your routine*

Most recovering sugar addicts, myself included, had pretty irregular meal schedules. We indulged our sugar cravings whenever we wanted to, often eating only one or two real meals a day and several huge calorie bomb snacks in between.

So stay disciplined by breaking that cycle. Don't skip your meals. I've included plenty of super-fast, microwavable snacks and even complete meals you can whip up in less than two minutes and enjoy on the go. So there's no excuse. By the way, I can't wait to hear from you about any variations you create or new substitutions you discover!

How To Avoid Sugar When Eating Out

Restaurants

Naturally, if you're dining in a restaurant you can't control the menu, but that's no reason to avoid going out and having fun.

If you're going to a chain restaurant or any place that has their menu online, take two minutes to research the menu and plan out what you want beforehand. Besides decreasing the chance you'll make a mistake and order something with hidden sugar inside, your meal mates will be pleasantly surprised to see the supposed "picky eater" in the group ready to order before them.

If you don't have to time to plan ahead and/or the menu doesn't include any nutrition information, speak up. I've even gone so far as to have the staff pull the books out to show me precisely how much sugar is in something on the menu. It's second nature now. All I can say is I will not go back to my old ways. This is most definitely a lifestyle change and not some passing fad.

If you're not the sort to make a fuss, you'll still be okay by just following a few simple guidelines.

➢ Skip the bread appetizer. Ask the waiter to bring your salad out early if you're starving or request a vegetable platter instead of bread.

➢ If you can't find any dish that appeals to you while not having too many starches or added sugars, then just ask for a switcheroo. See if they can swap the fries, potatoes, rice or noodles with some spinach, steamed vegetables or whatever similar starch-free ingredients you're in the mood for. This is rarely a problem for the restaurant, since the vegies are generally cheaper than the items you're replacing and they're going to charge you the same price anyway.

➢ Always ask for every item to be grilled or oven-baked, rather than fried. Even if the entrée itself is low-carb, who knows what sort of oil the cook is using.

➢ If everything is tasting bland, butter is always a safe flavor topping. It has no sugar and no carbs in it, plus butter fits with just about everything (at least to us Southerners). You can also just ask for a side of olive oil and vinegar.

➢ To avoid hidden sugars, the biggest thing you should watch out for are condiments and sauces. But so many eateries love to slather their main dishes in various sauces, gravies and all sorts of sugar-rich coverings. A lot of the time that's intended to mask the poor taste of the low-quality and past-its-prime meat, but that's a subject for another book. The point is, always double check if your entrée comes with any type of condiment and ask for it on the side. That's a quick and simple compromise, and the waiters usually just grin when I ask for my meat "dry."

➢ If everyone's ordering a dessert and you're feeling tempted, try a simple bowl of strawberries, blueberries or raspberries with heavy cream. That's quite low carb and most restaurants should be able to accommodate you.

Dinner parties and other social functions

I understand that these can feel awkward. You don't want to annoy your host with a long list of dietary requirements, nor spend the whole time trying to explain why you can't eat this or that.

If you can't prepare your own dish ahead of time, just eat beforehand. Don't make it complicated.

Emergency Situations

So what do you do if you left the house early in a rush? No time for breakfast. You didn't bring your healthy snacks. You've got a stressful day ahead and you're starving already. Oh, and you've only got five bucks in your pocket to last you until payday.

It's tempting to snatch some cheap heart attack in a sack from a fast food joint on your way to work. Maybe you'll even promise yourself you won't crash on the couch when you get home and you'll get some extra exercise in tonight. Maybe you actually have the discipline to do that, but why gamble with your health?

Just stop at a gas station and put that five dollars to work with some high protein snacks that will keep you full all day, rather than a quick sugar rush that will fade in an hour. Granted, most of these gas station snacks are fairly high fat and high sodium, but that's a far smaller concern than staying away from extra sugar. Remember, we're not planning the perfect meal, but rather dealing with an emergency situation that would otherwise lead you to backslide into the treacherous arms of sugar.

Some of my favorite cheap and hasty meals are natural beef jerky, sunflower seeds (without sugar flavorings), peanuts, pork skins, cheese and popped sorghum, or sugar-free popcorn.

Miscellaneous Money Saving Tips

With this lifestyle change, you're already saving a small fortune by avoiding fast-food, junk food and sugary drinks. Simply giving up the empty-calorie junk is usually enough to ensure you can afford the things that are good for your body. But you can save even more money with just a few tweaks to your shopping habits:

- If money is tight, buy frozen vegetables instead of fresh or canned. Yes, fresh is usually the best, but also the most expensive.

- Don't buy the precut or prepackaged vegetables. Get a whole cauliflower or whole broccoli and cut it yourself. Even if that's more than you need, you can always freeze what you are not going to eat and pull out when needed. Plus, having to push aside a mound of veggies in the fridge every time you reach for something sugary is a great way to help you stick to your diet goals.

- Stock up on meat when it's on sale. Doesn't matter if this is more than you need because it won't go to waste. When that beef, chicken, pork etc hits it's sell-by date and the store marks the price down by 33% or more, that's too good a deal to miss out on. You're basically getting three meals for the price of two. You can go ahead and cook several days' worth of meat at once, saving you a ton of time later, then freeze whatever's left over. Personally, I usually plan my next three days of meals according to whatever is on sale at the grocery store when I'm there.

- The same goes doubly true for cheese, since we're staying away from processed poison and only eating expensive organic cheeses. Contrary to common belief, you can freeze any type of cheese without any significant loss of flavor. Just make sure you chop or shred the big block first to reduce crumbling. Then thaw it in the fridge instead of in the sink.

- Some cheeses, like feta, you may want to freeze as a block. Feta crumbles quite easily after being frozen. Feta is usually significantly cheaper per ounce by the block vs. already crumbled.

- Thrift stores are great places to buy cheap these specialty cooking aides that you won't use every day. Such as a cake pop maker, doughnut maker or whoopie pie maker. Not to mention all sorts of ultra-expensive electric blender accessories for a fraction of the retail price.

How To Create Tasty, Sugar Free Versions Of Any Recipe

Natural Sugar Substitutes

Replacing Refined Sugar with Natural Sugar Substitutes

Amount of processed sugar in original recipe:	1 teaspoon	1 tablespoon	1/2 cup	1 cup
Sugar Alternative:				
Allulose	1 teaspoon	1 tablespoon	1/2 cup	1.25 cups
Isomalt	1 teaspoon	1 tablespoon	1/2 cup	1 cup
Monk Fruit Blends	1 teaspoon	1 tablespoon	1/2 cup	1 cup
Splenda (liquid)	1 drop	3 drops	1/4 teaspoon	1/2 teaspoon
Splenda (powder)	1 teaspoon	1 tablespoon	1/2 cup	1 cup
Stevia (liquid)	2-4 drops	6 - 9 drops	1/2 teaspoon	1 teaspoon
Stevia (pure extract)	pinch (1/16 teaspoon)	1/4 teaspoon	1/2 teaspoon	1 teaspoon
Stevia Blends	1 teaspoon	1 tablespoon	1/2 cup	1 cup
Swerve	1 teaspoon	1 tablespoon	1/2 cup	1 cup
Tagatose	1 teaspoon	1 tablespoon	1/2 cup	1 cup
Truvia	1/2 teaspoon	1/2 tablespoon	1/4 cub	1/2 cup
Xylitol	1 teaspoon	1 tablespoon	1/2 cup	1 cup
Z-Sweet	1 teaspoon	1 tablespoon	1/2 cup	1 cup

46

Birch Sugar (Xylitol)

This sugar alcohol is by far my favorite. Xylitol has only 40% the calories of regular sugar. It's reasonably priced and incredibly easy to replace sugar in any type of recipe. Another great benefit is it doesn't have that artificial aftertaste you find with so many other sweeteners.

Note for pet owners: While Xylitol is perfectly safe for human consumption, it is extremely toxic to dogs. So please make sure your pet doesn't get into your leftovers. Even small amounts of xylitol can cause hypoglycemia (low blood sugar), seizures, liver failure or even death in dogs.[28]

Stevia-Sweetened Dark Chocolate

While there are many types of sugar-free dark chocolates to choose from, most still have that distinctive bitter taste that many people don't like. In my opinion, a great compromise is any dark chocolate sweetened with Stevia. These have a much milder taste than normal high-cacao dark chocolate and more closely match the flavor of traditional semi-sweet baking chocolate. Carefully read the labels on these brands, of course, but most of the time they're 100% sugar free and ultra-low carb.

Note On Making Sugar-Free Soda Without Artificial Sweeteners.

When making your own soda, you want to use a simple syrup-based sweetener. I recommend xylitol or stevia. Then you can mix with sparkling water and don't need any sort of special equipment to make your soft drinks.

How to Work With Gluten-Free Flour Blends

Swapping out gluten-free flour is crucial to staying sugar free, even if you don't have Celiac disease. If you're trying to lose weight, on any diet, you need to cut down that massive load of unneeded carbs you find in wheat products. The best part though is experimenting with these flours lets you create low carb versions of all your favorite foods.

So here are some mix ratios to get you started. Remember to always use extra eggs and binders when using gluten-free anything. Add even more if you're baking something that needs to rise.

As a rule of thumb, I'll use 15% more binding (such as xanthan gum or guar-gum) than the recipe calls for and then adjust as necessary. If the end result is too fluffy or crumbling, then cut back on the egg and binding agent. If the final product is too dense or just won't

---

[28] Pet Poison Helpline. "Xylitol Toxicity in Dogs." https://vcahospitals.com/know-your-pet/xylitol-toxicity-in-dogs

rise, add more. While the first batch might not be perfect this way, it's close enough that no one is going to turn up their nose and back away from your table.

To replace 1 cup of white flour in your recipe, you can use the following flour combos and ratios:

- ¾ cup Almond flour
- ¼ Almond flour cup + ½ cup Coconut flour
- 1 cup Coconut flour
- 3/4 cup Coconut flour + ¼ cup Sorghum flour
- ½ cup Green banana flour + ½ cup Coconut flour
- ¼ cup Garbanzo bean flour + ½ cup Almond flour + ¼ cup Oat fiber
- ¼ cup Sorghum flour + ¼ cup Einkorn flour + ¼ cup oat fiber

Note: There is gluten in the einkorn flour, but that's one of the less common combinations. This whole thing is not an exact science. There are so many things that can play a role in your baking and cooking, such as humidity and cold temperatures, but these are the things that work for me.

Use sparkling water instead of tap water.

One of the biggest problems when baking with nut-based ingredients instead of gluten-based flour is getting things to rise properly in the oven. Through much trial and error, I've discovered that sparkling water will activate the baking powder and create the rise you need. At least in every recipe I've tested. Perhaps there are more professional activating agents you can try, but sparkling water is cheap and readily available just about everywhere.

Aluminum-free baking powder.

This is optional, but I strongly recommend sticking to aluminum-free baking powder in every recipe. This will keep you from getting that strange metallic taste.

One note though: The metal-free version of baking soda reacts mainly to liquid and not to heat. So if you take too long between mixing the batter and putting your cake in the oven, the chemical reaction will have petered out and you won't get as much of a rise. On the plus side, your food won't taste like a hubcap.

Natural Starchy Carbohydrate Replacements

There are so many options to replace potatoes, rice and white bread—the big three empty carb bombs. I'll cover all the details in the appropriate recipes, but here are the general ingredients you can use to replace all those high carb ingredients in any recipe, while still keeping the same taste and texture.

Almond Flour

When it comes to wheat and gluten substitutes, nothing beats the flavor, versatility and reasonable pricing of almond flour. It's also incredibly healthy, with only 6 grams of carbs per 28 gram serving, and half of that comes from dietary fiber. There's even compelling evidence that almond flour helps lower cholesterol and blood pressure.[29]

Best of all, it's incredibly easy to swap white flour with almond flour, thereby cutting out the bulk of carbs from any recipe. I've yet to come across a single recipe where I couldn't substitute almond flour cup for cup with all-purpose (white) flour, and still come out with a result that closely matches not just the flavor but also the texture of the original.

Note: Almond *meal* is made by grinding almonds with their skins intact, which is much coarser than almond flour. That's a great substitute for corn meal, but don't use almond meal to replace any type of flour.

Garbanzo Bean Flour (Chickpeas)

For those people with a nut allergy, garbanzo bean flour is an affordable, tasty and easy to use alternative to white flour. This is the same high-protein, high-fiber and gluten-free chickpeas used to make hummus, just ground into a fine powder. While there are natural sugars in this, about 10% by weight, it's still a much better alternative than white flour. For every cup of chickpea flour, you're looking at a net 43 grams of non-fiber carbs, versus 91 grams of non-fiber carbohydrates for every cup of all-purpose flour.

When substituting for all-purpose flour, use ¾ as much garbanzo bean flour as the recipe calls for all-purpose flour. Like with almond flour, there isn't a major difference in flavor or texture compared to wheat flour. Again though, include around 15% more binding agent than the recipe calls for to compensate for the lack of gluten and then adjust as needed.

Oat Fiber (not to be confused with oat flour)

From a nutrition standpoint, oat fiber is the next best gluten-free and non-nut alternative to almond flour. It is zero carb, free of natural sugar and loaded with fiber. The last is quite important since it can be troublesome to get enough fiber when following a low-carb diet.

---

[29] Finegold, J., Asaria, P., and Francisa, D. (2013). *Mortality From Ischaemic Heart Disease By Country, Region, And Age: Statistics From World Health Organisation And United Nations.* *H*ttps://www.ncbi.nlm.nih.gov/pmc/articles/PMC3819990/

The only downsides are that oat fiber can't completely replace white flour and takes a little more experimentation to make it fit just right into different recipes. It acts like white flour. And it is a great filler when making cakes, bread, cookies, pancakes, meat loaf… it adds extra fiber which we all need without the sugar or the carbs.

Note: With recipes requiring baking powder, add 2 1/2 teaspoons baking powder per cup of oat flour. If the recipe calls for buttermilk, replace the buttermilk with 1/2 teaspoon of baking soda for each cup of milk.

Coconut flour

For those with a nut allergy or looking for extra sweetness, coconut flour is a great option. It's also one of the most fiber-dense flours out there and features heavily in my baked goods recipes.

Lupin beans Flour

Another sugar-free and nut-free option. This flour has a flexible texture you can use anywhere.

Green banana flour

Green banana flower is made from dried green bananas. While it does have some sugar, it's still incredibly low carb. It has a very mild banana flavor too.

Use Cauliflower or jicama instead of potatoes

Cauliflower is exceptionally low in calories and carbs. Best of all, when mashed up it matches the texture of potatoes with a slightly sweeter taste. You can also chop or rice it to replace short-grained rice, macaroni noodles and even grits in any recipe. Cauliflower also cooks faster than potatoes and needs less prep time, since you don't have to peel a thing.

I recently started experimenting with the jicama root vegetable. Often called the "Mexican turnip." It has the texture of a potato without needing to be mashed first, and it tastes a bit sweeter

There is a little bit of starch inside jicama, but if that's a problem, you can cook it first and then soak it in cold water for a little while to extract most of the starch.

Sample One Week Meal Plan

Meal plan day 1

Breakfast:

Spinach Bacon egg cheese *breakfast* sandwich

Lunch:

4 cup spring mix salad with 12 blueberries, ¼ cup Blue cheese crumbles, 12 almonds, ¼ cup red onion, 4 olives, 3 ounces meat (tuna, Chicken, Beef, Pork)

Vinegar and oil dressing.

Dinner:

4 ounces pork tenderloin with grated onion and minced garlic on top, 1cup steamed Broccoli, ¼ wedge of iceberg lettuce with 2 cherry tomatoes cut in half, dressing made of 2 tablespoons sour cream, 1 teaspoon of your favorite spice blend (one without sugar), black pepper.

Meal plan day 2

Breakfast:

2 scrambled eggs, three slices of bacon, 2 ounces of cheese melted with 1 tablespoon heavy whipping cream poured over the spinach, 2 cups of spinach seasoned with butter, sugar-free seasoning blend and bone broth..

Lunch:

4 cups Spring mix salad, three strawberries cubed into 12 or more pieces, ¼ cup feta cheese,

10 pecans, 3 ounces of cubed chicken. ½ teaspoon of raspberry blush glaze and 2 tablespoons of white wine vinegar. Salt and pepper to taste.

Dinner:

Steamed fish 4 oz, 2 cups of collards (no sugar added), 1 almond flour corn essence muffin.

Meal plan day 3

Breakfast: 3 almond flour pancakes, yacon syrup, 3 slices of bacon,

Lunch:

2 cups Broccoli cheddar soup, almond flour bread croutons

Dinner:

Shirataki noodles with sugar free marinara sauce, beef meatballs, parmesan cheese, 3 cups of spring mix salad, olives, onion, peppers, cubed mozzarella cheese, cubed salami, oil and vinegar dressing.

Meal plan day 4

Breakfast:

Shrimp and grits, 1 donut hole

Lunch:

4 cups Spring mix salad with ¼ cup grated carrots, onion, pickle, 3 grape tomatoes, 2 oz

Crumbled cheddar cheese, 3 ounces chicken, low sugar dressing of choice

Dinner:

Grilled fish, collards, chopped egg with onion and celery and swiss cheese.

Meal plan day 5

Breakfast:

Spinach, Sausage, mushroom omelet, 1 slice almond flour toast, butter and blueberry jelly.

Lunch:

4 cups mixed greens, radish, chopped boiled egg, cubed ham, cheddar cheese, chopped pickle, crumbled bacon, chopped onion with sour cream heavy whipping cream dill spice dressing.

Dinner:

Beef and Broccoli stir fry with almonds and sesame seeds, cabbage carrot slaw, almond flour Choco cake.

Meal plan day 6

Breakfast:

2 Scrambled eggs, 3 slices bacon, Radish hash browns, 1 slice almond flour toast with butter and sugar free strawberry jelly

Lunch:

Pork skin nacho salad, mixed greens, onion, red, green, yellow orange peppers, low sugar salsa,

White cheese queso, ground beef, sour cream, green olives

Dinner:

Pork fried rice, Zucchini and onion sauté, 2 coconut flour butter cookies

Meal plan day 7

Breakfast:

Sausage biscuit and gravy, 1 egg, 1 cup spinach

Lunch:

Broccoli chicken wrap with pumpkin turmeric chips and hummus

Dinner:

Steak and mashed cauliflower potatoes, green beans with truffle oil, almond flour chocolate chip cookie

Recipes

Most of these recipes are sugar and starch free, but some do include a small amount of sugar and carbs. Not a single meal will break your sugar budget though.

Just as important, I've focused on fast and cheap meals. There are fancier ingredients you could use and more elaborate preparation styles that might improve flavor somewhat, but I'm assuming most folks don't have the time, resources nor patience to spend in the kitchen every single day.

I have always loved to cook and would create elaborate meals for my family. I am now learning a new way to cook that fits my sugar free lifestyle change. There are more recipes out there than I can count. These recipes are some of my favorites and my family's new favorites that I have either created myself or tweaked to fit my sugar free lifestyle. I hope you find these recipes to be easy to make with not a lot of ingredients and not a lot of experience.

Breakfast

EGGS FLORENTINE BISCUIT W/ HAM & CHEESE

Servings	Prep Time	Cook Time
4	10 mins	2 mins

Create your biscuits using my Homemade Biscuit recipe.

INGREDIENTS

- ✓ 3 eggs
- ✓ 1 teaspoon butter
- ✓ 1 cup spinach, frozen or fresh
- ✓ 1 teaspoon of your favorite spice blend that does not contain sugar or salt, preferably with a citrus flavor
- ✓ 2 pinches black pepper
- ✓ pinch of cayenne pepper or spicy paprika
- ✓ 2 tablespoons heavy whipping cream
- ✓ 2 ounces sliced ham (enough for 4 biscuits)
- ✓ 2 ounces sliced cheddar cheese or cheese of your choice (enough for 4 biscuits)
- ✓ 4 homemade biscuits

DIRECTIONS

1) Crack 3 eggs in a bowl, holding out one yoke in a separate glass microwave safe container.
2) Grease a microwave safe plate or pan with butter. Whisk your eggs, then pour onto the plate or pan. Cook your eggs on the microwave-safe plate for 120 seconds or in a pan. On the stove.
3) When the microwave eggs cool, cut them into 4 equal pieces.
4) In a skillet, add ½ teaspoon butter, 1 cup of spinach, spice blend, pepper and cayenne. Cook until the spinach is wilted.
5) Whisk the single egg yolk, cheese and the heavy whipping cream in a small microwave safe container. Microwave at 5 second intervals for 20 seconds, stirring at every interval. This will ensure the raw egg is cooked. You will have a lovely Florentine like sauce.
6) Open your biscuit and add a little sauce, then add one of the egg slices, cooked spinach and sliced ham. Add more sauce then put the top back on your biscuit.

BREAKFAST TORTILLA WRAP

Servings	Prep Time	Cook Time
4	5 mins	5 mins

Create the tortillas using my Ultra-Low Carb Tortillas recipe.

Variations: These are quick and easy, and the variations are endless. Create several in advance and keep frozen for the days you need a quick breakfast.

INGREDIENTS

- ✓ 4 eggs
- ✓ 1 teaspoon butter
- ✓ ¼ cup red or green bell peppers
- ✓ ¼ cup sweet onions
- ✓ pinch black pepper
- ✓ 3 ounces cheese (any kind)
- ✓ 2 tablespoons heavy whipping cream

DIRECTIONS

1) Place the butter, peppers, onions and black pepper in the skillet. Sauté for 2 minutes.

2) Whisk the eggs and the heavy whipping cream together. Pour over the hot pepper and onion in the skillet.

3) Turn heat off, eggs will continue to cook.

4) Add the cheese.

5) Divide egg pepper mixture into four equal amounts. Put on center of tortillas. Roll it up enjoy.

BAKED CAULIFLOWER GRITS CASSEROLE

Servings	Prep Time	Cook Time
8	10 mins	10 mins

Variations: add peppers and onions, Sprinkle cooked bacon on top.

Tip: If it is overcooked, melt 1 cup of cheese and 3 tablespoons of heavy whipping cream in the microwave and pour over the top.

INGREDIENTS

- ✓ 6 eggs
- ✓ 4 cups shredded cauliflower (riced)
- ✓ 1 lb. Cooked sausage (cooled)
- ✓ 2 cups cheddar cheese
- ✓ ½ cup heavy whipping cream
- ✓ 2 vegetable bouillon cubes
- ✓ 1 tablespoon of your favorite spice blend

DIRECTIONS

1) Mix the eggs and cream until solid color then add everything else.

2) Pour into a buttered or parchment paper lined 12" casserole dish.

3) Bake 350° for 20-25 minutes.

4) Look for the doneness of the egg in the center. The casserole will continue to cook when pulled out of the oven.

BREAKFAST GRITS BOWL

Servings	Prep Time	Cook Time
4	5 mins	6 mins

Variations: hot sauce, gravy, jelly or cheese spoon on top.

INGREDIENTS

- ✓ 2 cups finely ground cauliflower (see my instructions)
- ✓ ½ cup of water
- ✓ 1 tablespoon of butter
- ✓ ¼ Salt
- ✓ Pepper to taste
- ✓ ½ cube chicken bouillon or beef
- ✓ ½ cup Heavy whipping cream or milk
- ✓ 2 scrambled eggs
- ✓ ¼ cup Chopped bacon ham sausage

DIRECTIONS

1) In a saucepan place the cauliflower, 1 tablespoon of butter, the bouillon cube, Salt and Pepper. Sauté for two minutes stirring constantly.

2) Add your water and cook for an additional six minutes stirring so that it doesn't stick. Turn your heat down to simmer at this time.

3) Add heavy whipping cream. Cook 1 or 2 minutes depending on the thickness you like. (some people like grits soupier) turn the heat off. Remove from heat.

4) Scoop grits onto a plate or bowl. Place two spoons of scrambled eggs in the center of the spooned grits. Sprinkle chopped bacon or ham or sausage. Add any other toppings you would like. I like cheese.

CHEESE AND HAM CUP – MICROWAVEABLE

Servings	Prep Time	Cook Time
4	5 mins	1 min

INGREDIENTS

- ✓ 2 eggs
- ✓ 1 tablespoon dried rosemary
- ✓ 1 teaspoon yellow mustard
- ✓ ½ cup sour cream
- ✓ 1/3 cup walnut oil
- ✓ ¼ cup finely shredded Parmesan cheese
- ✓ ½ cup finely shredded cheddar cheese
- ✓ ½ cup almond flour
- ✓ 4 tablespoons oat fiber
- ✓ 4 tablespoons sorghum flour
- ✓ 1 tablespoon baking powder (aluminum free)
- ✓ 4 ounces chopped ham, sausage or bacon

DIRECTIONS

1) Mix oil, sour cream, Rosemary and mustard for one minute, then add the eggs and cheeses.

2) In a separate bowl combine almond flour, oat fiber, sorghum flour and baking powder whisk together.

3) Add half the dry ingredients to the wet mix for one minute at the remainder dry ingredients mix another minute add the ham.

4) Place parchment paper in a microwavable safe loaf pan or coffee cup. Fill half full and microwave for 60 seconds.

EGG SPINACH BACON BREAKFAST SANDWICH

Servings	Prep Time	Cook Time
4	5 mins	1 min

They can also be made ahead of time. I make double batches and freeze them. You can microwave for 30 seconds and eat it on the way to work or school.

Variations: Kale instead of spinach, Ham or beef patty instead of bacon.

INGREDIENTS

- ✓ Almond flour muffin
- ✓ 2 cups fresh Spinach
- ✓ 4 Eggs (scrambled or microwave cooked)
- ✓ 4 slices Cheese (or 3 ounces melted)
- ✓ 4 slices cooked Bacon (break into 2 pieces each)

DIRECTIONS

1) 4 almond flour muffins (see recipe page)

2) You can cook the eggs quickly in the microwave. Crack the egg on a parchment paper lined plate. Break the yoke with a fork and swirl around. Do not over stir. Microwave for 60 seconds.

3) Cut apart and add spinach, egg, cheese and Bacon.

4) Warm sandwiches for 10 seconds in the microwave.

BISCUIT W/ HAM & CHEESE

Servings	Prep Time	Cook Time
4	5 mins	1 min

Use biscuit from my previous biscuit recipe keep frozen until needed.

INGREDIENTS

- ✓ 4 eggs (scrambled or microwave cooked)
- ✓ 4 slices of Ham cooked (sugar free)
- ✓ 4 slices of cheese (or 3 ounces melted)
- ✓ 4 Biscuits

DIRECTIONS

1) Crack the egg on a parchment paper lined plate. Break the yoke with a fork and swirl around. Do not over stir.

2) Microwave for 60 seconds.

3) Add toppings and microwave until cheese is melted.

SPINACH MUSHROOM CHEESE OMELET

Servings	Prep Time	Cook Time
4	5 mins	2 mins

Use biscuit from my previous biscuit recipe keep frozen until needed. Variations: Melt cheese and pour over the top. Add meat. Replace spinach with kale.

INGREDIENTS

- ✓ 3 eggs
- ✓ 3 tablespoons heavy whipping cream
- ✓ ¼ teaspoon salt
- ✓ 2 pinches pepper
- ✓ ½ teaspoon butter
- ✓ 2 cup spinach frozen or fresh (seasoned to taste)
- ✓ 1 cup sliced mushrooms
- ✓ 1 cup extra sharp cheddar cheese

DIRECTIONS

1) Cook the spinach and mushrooms together and set aside.

2) Whisk the eggs and heavy whipping cream until a solid color.

3) In a nonstick skillet, heat butter until light brown on med heat. Add the egg.

4) Do not stir the egg. Swirl the pan until the egg is spread out as far as it can before it stops running. Turn the heat off. Sprinkle the cheese over all the egg.

5) Add the salt, pepper, spinach and mushrooms to one ½ of the egg. Tilt the pan and use a large spatula to fold the ½ of the egg that has no spinach and mushroom over the half that has the mushroom and spinach.

6) Slide out of the pan and cut into 4 sections.

SPICY BREAKFAST WRAP

Servings	Prep Time	Cook Time
4	5 mins	5 mins

Use wraps from my previous recipe. Keep frozen until needed. Variation: Spoon some extra salsa on top of the wrap. Add some cauliflower grits.

Add jalapenos. Add taco sauce (sugar free).

INGREDIENTS

- ✓ 3 eggs scrambled
- ✓ 2 tablespoons heavy whipping cream
- ✓ ½ teaspoon butter
- ✓ 1 cup shredded cheese (any flavor cheese)
- ✓ ½ cup of salsa (no sugar added)
- ✓ 1 cup of sausage (precooked)
- ✓ 4 Tortilla wraps (sugar free)

DIRECTIONS

1) Whisk eggs and heavy whipping cream. Scramble the eggs in a skillet with the butter. Add the sausage, egg, cheese and salsa. Divide into 4 equal parts.

2) Place the mixture on tortillas and roll up. Microwave for 10 seconds with a dampened unprinted paper towel on top.

SCRAMBLED EGGS WITH COLLARDS

Servings	Prep Time	Cook Time
4	10 mins	10 mins

Variations: Spinach instead of collards. Bacon instead of ham. Spicy seasoning instead of original. Add hot sauce.

INGREDIENTS

- ✓ 3 eggs
- ✓ ½ teaspoon butter
- ✓ 1 tablespoon walnut oil (any oil will do)
- ✓ 3 tablespoons heavy whipping cream
- ✓ ¼ cup chopped ham
- ✓ 4 cups chopped collards
- ✓ ½ cup chopped onions
- ✓ 1 tablespoon any salt free seasoning
- ✓ 1 vegetable bouillon cube
- ✓ ½ teaspoon salt
- ✓ 3 tablespoons water

DIRECTIONS

1) Use a cast iron skillet or saucepan medium heat. Place the oil, onion and ham. Cook for 3 minutes. Stirring constantly. Start adding handfuls of the collards. Add until all are in the pot. Stirring constantly. Turn the heat to low. Add the seasoning, bouillon cube (crumbled) and water if needed.

2) Whisk the eggs and heavy whipping cream. Pour into the hot collards and put a lid on top. Turn the heat off. After 1-minute lift the lid off and fold the eggs into the collards. The steam from the collards cooks the eggs. The more you fold the eggs the greener they become.

3) Tip: Chopping collards, lay 5 collards on top of each other and roll tight. Cut in ¼ inch lengths. Then cut into 2-inch lengths.

GREEN BANANA FLOUR WAFFLES/PANCAKES

Servings	Prep Time	Cook Time
6	10 mins	10 mins

Variations: Chocolate chips, blueberries, Raspberries, coconut.

INGREDIENTS

- ✓ ¾ cup green banana flour
- ✓ ¼ cup oat fiber
- ✓ 2 teaspoon baking powder (aluminum free)
- ✓ 3 eggs
- ✓ ½ cup of sparkling water
- ✓ 4 tablespoons birch xylitol
- ✓ 1 teaspoon of vanilla
- ✓ ½ tablespoon apple cider vinegar
- ✓ 1 tablespoon butter
- ✓ 1 tablespoon sour cream

DIRECTIONS

1) Preheat your waffle iron or your skillet if you're doing pancakes. Combine your dry ingredients in a medium-sized bowl and set that aside

2) Now put all your wet ingredients except the sparkling water in a mixer and mix for two minutes

3) Whisk the dry ingredients into the wet mixture.

4) Mix 1 minute. Add your sparkling water. Mix it well. Pour into your waffle iron or make pancakes on a griddle.

SHRIMP AND CAULIFLOWER GRITS

Servings	Prep Time	Cook Time
6	8 mins	6 mins

This is a low sugar substitute for traditional shrimp and grits. Variations: Pan fry cauliflower mixed with 1 tablespoon oat fiber in 2 tablespoons of oil to give it a bit of a crunch.

CAULIFLOWER GRITS

- ✓ 1 head of cauliflower (4 cups riced)
- ✓ 1/2 cup heavy whipping cream
- ✓ 2 tablespoons butter
- ✓ ½ teaspoon salt
- ✓ ½ teaspoon pepper
- ✓ 3/4 cup chicken stock or bone broth
- ✓ ½ cup grated sharp cheddar cheese

DIRECTIONS

1) Grade or use a food processor to rice the cauliflower.

2) Cook cauliflower in skillet with butter and chicken stock salt and pepper for 6 to 8 minutes. Pull ½ the cauliflower out. Use an immersion blender to purée the cauliflower in the skillet. Add the ½ of pulled out cauliflower back in. Add the rest of the ingredients. Stir and set aside.

SPICY SHRIMP

- ✓ 1 tablespoon of your favorite hot and spicy seasoning blend (one without sugar and salt)
- ✓ 3 slices bacon
- ✓ 1 teaspoon minced garlic
- ✓ ¼ cup chopped onion
- ✓ ¼ cup chopped green pepper
- ✓ 1lb of peeled shrimp

DIRECTIONS

1) In a skillet, cook bacon. Add the minced garlic, onion, green pepper, and shrimp.

2) Stir and cook until shrimp turn pink add the spicy seasoning and salt.

3) Put the spicy shrimp on the grits, serve hot.

4) Optional: Marinade the cauliflower overnight with cream and spices. This adds an extra level of flavor.

OAT FIBER PANCAKE RECIPE

Servings	Prep Time	Cook Time
6	10 mins	10 mins

Variations: Add blueberries, chocolate chips or side of bacon

INGREDIENTS

- ✓ 1/2 cup oat fiber
- ✓ ¼ cup almond flour
- ✓ 2 tablespoons sour cream
- ✓ 1 teaspoon unsweetened unflavored gelatin
- ✓ 3 tablespoons walnut oil
- ✓ 3 tablespoons birch xylitol
- ✓ 1 tablespoon aluminum free baking powder
- ✓ 2 tablespoons sparkling water
- ✓ 1 tablespoon butter
- ✓ 1 egg

DIRECTIONS

1) Mix all ingredients except the sparkling water together for 2 minutes.

2) Add the water and stir well.

3) Heat griddle add butter pour batter and cook.

ALMOND FLOUR MUFFINS

Servings	Prep Time	Cook Time
6	6 mins	12 mins

Tip: use a whoopie pie maker or whoopie pie pan to make perfect shaped muffins.

INGREDIENTS

- ✓ 1 cup almond flour
- ✓ ½ cup coconut flour
- ✓ 2 teaspoons Unflavored Unsweetened Gelatin
- ✓ ½ cup walnut oil
- ✓ ½ cup butter or ghee
- ✓ 1 tablespoon of your favorite spice blend (one without sugar and salt)
- ✓ 1 tablespoon aluminum free baking powder
- ✓ 2 eggs
- ✓ 4 tablespoons unsweetened sparkling water

DIRECTIONS

1) Mix the oil, butter and seasoning for two minutes.

2) Add coconut flour, almond flour, gelatin and eggs, then mix well.

3) Mix baking powder and sparkling water in a tall glass. Add to the mixture quickly.

4) Bake at 350° for 12 minutes.

MICROWAVABLE CHEDDAR BACON BISCUITS

Servings	Prep Time	Cook Time
2	5 mins	2 min

Variations: Add 1tablespoon of jalapenos, onions, ham and swiss cheese or sausage

INGREDIENTS

- ✓ 2 tablespoons butter
- ✓ 2 tablespoons coconut flour
- ✓ 2 tablespoons almond flour
- ✓ 1tablespoon aluminum free baking powder
- ✓ 1 egg
- ✓ 1-ounce grated cheddar cheese
- ✓ 1 slice of bacon crisp and crumbled
- ✓ 1 teaspoon of your favorite spice blend
- ✓ 2 tablespoons sparkling water

DIRECTIONS

1) Mix everything together for 1 minute.

2) Butter a 2-cup glass measuring cup and microwave for 90 seconds.

3) Wait 30 seconds and flip it out onto a plate.

4) Wait another minute and then you can slice it.

HOMEMADE BISCUITS

Servings	Prep Time	Cook Time
6-8	10 mins	12 mins

INGREDIENTS

- ✓ ¼ cup butter
- ✓ ¼ cup walnut oil
- ✓ ¼ cup coconut flour
- ✓ ½ cup almond flour
- ✓ 3 tablespoons sorghum flour
- ✓ 3 tablespoons oat fiber
- ✓ 1 tablespoon baking powder
- ✓ 1 tablespoon of your favorite spice blend
- ✓ 1 egg

DIRECTIONS

1) Mix all ingredients together for 2 minutes.

2) Using a non-stick spray (or butter), oil a standard muffin pan. Fill the muffin cups up to ½ full.

3) Or drop spoonsful onto a parchment paper lined cookie sheet.

4) Bake at 375° for 12 minutes.

BISCUITS AND GRAVY

Servings	Prep Time	Cook Time
6-8	5 mins	5 mins

Create your biscuits using my Homemade Biscuit recipe.

Variations: Make the gravy without sausage. Sprinkle crumbled bacon on the top of your biscuits & gravy as the last step.

INGREDIENTS

- ✓ 1 pound of ground sausage
- ✓ ¼ cup cream cheese
- ✓ ½ cup heavy whipping cream
- ✓ ¼ cup water or milk
- ✓ ¼ cup bone broth or beef bouillon
- ✓ ½ teaspoon salt
- ✓ ¼ teaspoon pepper (add more later)
- ✓ 6-8 homemade biscuits (see previous recipe)

DIRECTIONS

1) Pan fry your sausage, keeping the fat in the pan. If desired, remove the oil from the sausage by patting with a paper towel.

2) Add the salt, pepper and bone broth. Turn down to medium heat.

3) While your sausage is frying, mix the heavy whipping cream and cream cheese in a glass bowl. When the sausage is done, whisk this mixture into your pan. If the cream cheese is cold you can microwave for 6-10 seconds to soften with your cream to make it easier to mix.

4) While at medium heat, add your milk or water. Stir constantly.

5) As the mixture begins to thicken, turn off the heat. The sausage gravy will continue to thicken as the heat dissipates. Add more water or milk as needed to maintain desired consistency.

6) Open each biscuit on a plate and add the desired amount of sausage gravy mix.

BREAKFAST CAULIFLOWER SQUARES

Servings	Prep Time	Cook Time
8	10 mins	25 mins

Variations: add sausage, bacon or cheese

Make ahead: Freeze baked toasts between layers of wax or parchment paper in an airtight container for up to 3 months.

INGREDIENTS

- ✓ 5 cups cauliflower florets (about 1 pound)
- ✓ 1 cup shredded cheddar cheese
- ✓ 1 large egg, beaten
- ✓ ¼ teaspoon ground pepper
- ✓ ¼ teaspoon salt
- ✓ 2 teaspoons favorite all-purpose spice

DIRECTIONS

1) Preheat oven to 425°F. Line one large baking sheet with parchment paper.

2) Place cauliflower in a food processor. Process until finely grated.

3) Transfer to a microwave-safe bowl. Cover loosely and microwave on High for 3 minutes. Let cool slightly.

4) Transfer the cauliflower to a clean kitchen towel and wring out excess moisture.

5) Return cauliflower to the bowl and stir in Cheddar, egg, spice, pepper and salt until thoroughly combined.

6) Using about ¼ cup cauliflower mixture, create eight 3-inch squares on the prepared baking sheet.

7) Bake until the cauliflower is browned and crispy around the edges, 22 to 25 minutes.

RASPBERRY DANISH

Servings	Prep Time	Cook Time
12	5 mins	30 mins

An egg bread Danish recipe that's super low in total carbs. It's a nice low carb treat to enjoy any time of day. Variations: Strawberry, blueberry, blackberry, cinnamon apple. Add nuts.

Tip: use a plastic zip bag with a corner cut off to pipe the cream.

INGREDIENTS

Raspberry Filling

- ✓ 8 ounces cream cheese
- ✓ 1 cup chopped raspberries
- ✓ 1 teaspoon unflavored gelatin
- ✓ 3 tablespoons Birch xylitol powdered
- ✓ 1/2 teaspoon vanilla
- ✓ 1 egg

Base Egg Dough:

- ✓ 4 eggs divided
- ✓ 1 tablespoon birch xylitol Powdered
- ✓ 3 ounces cream cheese softened
- ✓ 1/4 cup unflavored gelatin
- ✓ 1 tablespoon coconut flour optional
- ✓ 1/2 teaspoon cream of tartar

DIRECTIONS

1) Preheat oven to 325°. Line two baking sheets or pans with parchment paper.

2) Work on the filling first. In blender or coffee grinder, grind the raspberries.

3) Mix together cream cheese, birch, vanilla, egg, gelatin and raspberries. Transfer to plastic bag or pastry bag. Chill till needed.

4) Now for the egg dough. Separate egg whites and yolks into separate mixing bowls.

5) Add birch, cream cheese and gelatin to yolks. Stir in coconut flour. Mix until smooth.

6) Whip egg whites with cream of tartar until stiff peaks form.

7) Gently fold yolk mixture into beaten whites.

8) Spoon 6 mounds of the egg batter onto each prepared baking sheets (12 mounds total). Flatten each mound slightly.

9) Get the filling and pipe the raspberry cream onto the center of each egg dough circle.

10) Bake at 325°F for 20-30 minutes.

Soups

CAULIFLOWER SOUP

Servings	Prep Time	Cook Time
8	10 mins	10 mins

Variations: Sprinkle bacon, cheese, or onion on top.

INGREDIENTS

- ✓ 1 head of cauliflower
- ✓ 1 tablespoons butter
- ✓ 2 eggs
- ✓ ¼ cup of lemon juice
- ✓ ½ teaspoon salt
- ✓ ¼ teaspoon pepper
- ✓ 1 teaspoon arrowroot or gelatin

DIRECTIONS

1) Divide cauliflower into florets. Sauté in skillet with butter salt and pepper until soft.

2) Add one cup of water continue to cook.

3) Whisk two eggs in a bowl with the lemon juice and arrowroot or gelatin. When it's well mixed, pour the egg mixture slowly over the cauliflower. Stirring carefully for two minutes. It will thicken.

CHICKEN NOODLE SOUP

Servings	Prep Time	Cook Time
8	15 mins	20 mins

INGREDIENTS

- ✓ 1 1/2 lbs. of chicken thighs
- ✓ 1 teaspoon salt
- ✓ 1 teaspoon pepper
- ✓ 1 tablespoon poultry seasoning (any with no sugar or msg)
- ✓ 2 cups water (1 cup for chicken/ 1 cup for the soup)
- ✓ ½ cup celery
- ✓ ½ cup chopped carrots
- ✓ ½ cup chopped onions
- ✓ 1 tablespoon of your favorite sugar-free spice blend
- ✓ 2 tablespoons minced garlic
- ✓ 2 vegetable bouillon cubes
- ✓ 1 cup chicken broth or bone broth
- ✓ 1/3 cup heavy cream
- ✓ 1 tablespoon butter
- ✓ 2 tablespoons walnut oil
- ✓ 8 ounces shitake noodles (cut with a knife)

DIRECTIONS

1) Place the chicken, 1 cup of water, salt, pepper, poultry seasoning in the minute pot for 5 to 6 minutes.

2) In skillet add walnut oil, butter, celery, carrots, onion, garlic, salt, pepper. Sauté for 4 minutes. In 4-quart stock pot add the broth, water, spice and bouillon cubes cream and noodles. Boil for three minutes. Shred chicken and add to the pot.

3) Simmer for 10 minutes.

HOT "POTATO" COLLARD SOUP

Servings	Prep Time	Cook Time
6	10 mins	5 mins

Variations: add bacon when serving, add sour cream, Kale instead of collards, spinach

INGREDIENTS

- ✓ 1 lb. Mild Italian sausage (no casing)
- ✓ 2 tablespoons walnut oil
- ✓ ¾ cup water
- ✓ 2 tablespoons steak seasoning
- ✓ 2 cups rutabaga cubed instead of potatoes
- ✓ 1 cup chopped onion
- ✓ 1 cup fresh collards (chopped small)
- ✓ 1 cup heavy whipping cream
- ✓ 1 cup beef bone broth or chicken broth

DIRECTIONS

1) In a skillet put 2 tablespoons of walnut oil, sausage, onions and steak seasoning together. Cook until onions are done over low heat. Add the bone broth. Add the cubed rutabaga to coat in juice.

2) Turn the heat off, transfer to a minute pot, pressure cooker or slow cooker. Pour the water into the skillet to get all the good bits out and add to your cooker. Add the cream and collards. Stir till mixed well. Cook and enjoy.

3) Tip: Chopping collards, lay 5 collards on top of each other and roll tight. Cut in ¼ inch lengths. Then cut into 2-inch lengths.

KALE CHICKEN NOODLE SOUP

Servings	Prep Time	Cook Time
8	10 mins	6 mins

Variations: Spinach instead of kale. Broccoli instead of kale. Add mixed vegetables. Add carrots.

INGREDIENTS

- ✓ 1lb chicken thighs with bone in (can use boneless)
- ✓ 1 tablespoon chicken blend seasoning (salt free and sugar free)
- ✓ 2 cups of water
- ✓ 2 bouillon cubes vegetable or chicken (or one of each)
- ✓ 1 tablespoon of butter
- ✓ 3 cups fresh Kale (chopped)
- ✓ 1 12ounce package of Shiitake noodles (fettucine or spaghetti)
- ✓ ¼ cup heavy whipping cream
- ✓ 2 teaspoons garlic powder
- ✓ 1 teaspoon salt
- ✓ ½ teaspoon pepper

DIRECTIONS

1) Open the package of noodles. Wash in a colander. Cut into 3-inch lengths.

2) In a minute pot, pressure cooker or crockpot add all the ingredients. Stir well.

3) Cook in a minute pot for 5 minutes. Cook in a stove top pressure cooker 3 minutes. Cook in a crock pot for 5 hours on low.

4) Tip: add more water if you want more juice. This is a recipe that tastes better after it is refrigerated for several hours.

5) Tip: for the Shiitake noodles. Wash them several times. Add to a plastic zip bag with salt free spices and 3 tablespoons cream. They will absorb the flavors. This adds an extra level of flavor.

BROCCOLI CHEDDAR SOUP WITH HAM AND BACON

Servings	Prep Time	Cook Time
8	10 mins	15 ins

Variation: The more you stir the smoother it gets if you like chunks of broccoli don't over stir.

INGREDIENTS

- ✓ 4 cups broccoli florets
- ✓ ½ cup chopped onion
- ✓ 2 tablespoons minced garlic
- ✓ 2 tablespoons walnut oil
- ✓ 2 vegetable bouillon cubes (sugar free)
- ✓ 1 tablespoon of your favorite spice blend (no sugar included)
- ✓ 1 teaspoon salt
- ✓ 1 teaspoon black pepper
- ✓ 1 cup chicken broth or bone broth
- ✓ 2 tablespoon cream cheese
- ✓ 2 cups cheddar cheese
- ✓ ½ cup heavy whipping cream
- ✓ 1 cup cubed ham
- ✓ 4 slices of cooked bacon (garnish)

DIRECTIONS

1) In a skillet, place walnut oil, onion, garlic, seasoning blend, salt, pepper, bouillon cubes, and cubed ham.

2) Cook until onions are translucent 3 to 5 minutes stirring constantly. Add the bone broth. Add broccoli, stirring until mixed well.

3) Continue to cook for eight to 10 minutes or until broccoli is tender.

4) In microwave safe bowl add the cheese, heavy whipping cream and cream cheese

5) Microwave for 30 second intervals stirring in between until cheese mixture is melted.

6) Add to the broccoli and stir.

WHITE SAUCE SAUSAGE KALE CHILI

Servings	Prep Time	Cook Time
8	10 mins	5 mins

Tip: Espresso powder or dark chocolate makes the flavors more intense.

Variations: Garbanzo beans instead of black beans. Chicken instead of sausage.

Red chili seasoning instead of white. Bacon and sour cream topping. White Cheese.

INGREDIENTS

- ✓ 2 lbs. of pork and kale sausage
- ✓ 1 tablespoon walnut oil (any oil will do)
- ✓ ½ cup chopped onion
- ✓ 1 cup fresh chopped kale
- ✓ 1 package white chili mix (sugar free)
- ✓ 1 cup heavy whipping cream
- ✓ 2 cups water
- ✓ 1/2 teaspoon espresso powder (or ¼ teaspoon dark cocoa powder)
- ✓ 1 cup finely chopped cauliflower (smaller than riced)
- ✓ 1 teaspoon white pepper
- ✓ 1 cup black beans

DIRECTIONS

1) In a skillet or saucepan, add oil, sausage and onion. Cook until sausage is done.

2) Pour into a minute pot, pressure cooker or crock pot. Add the rest of the ingredients. Mix well.

3) Cook in a minute pot for 5 minutes. Cook in a pressure cooker for 4 minutes. In a crock pot for 4 hours on low.

CROCK POT SAUERKRAUT SOUP

Servings	Prep Time	Cook Time
6	15 mins	5 mins

Variations: Ham, beef, fish or chicken

INGREDIENTS

- ✓ 1 cup jicama, cut into 1/4-inch cubes
- ✓ 1-pound smoked kielbasa, cut into 1/2-inch cubes
- ✓ 1 can (32 ounces sugar free) sauerkraut, rinsed and drained
- ✓ 4 cups chicken broth
- ✓ ½ cup heavy whipping cream
- ✓ 1 cup sliced fresh mushrooms
- ✓ 1 cup cubed cooked chicken
- ✓ 1 cubed carrot
- ✓ ¼ cup sliced celery
- ✓ 2 tablespoons white vinegar
- ✓ 2 teaspoons dill weed
- ✓ 1/2 teaspoon pepper
- ✓ 3 pieces bacon, cooked (for topping)

DIRECTIONS

1) Combine all ingredients.

2) Cook in a minute pot for 5 minutes or a crockpot for 4 minutes or in a 5-qt slow cooker on high for 5-6 hours or until the vegetables are tender. Top with bacon.

Breads, Wraps and Pizza Crusts

ALMOND FLOUR BREAD GLUTEN FREE

Servings	Prep Time	Cook Time
12	10 mins	45 mins

INGREDIENTS

- ✓ 2 cup almond flour
- ✓ 4 tablespoon psyllium husk powder
- ✓ 3 tablespoons oat fiber
- ✓ 1 package of unflavored gelatin
- ✓ 1 tablespoon aluminum free baking powder
- ✓ 1 teaspoon salt
- ✓ 4 eggs large
- ✓ 5 tablespoons walnut oil
- ✓ 2 tablespoon apple cider vinegar
- ✓ ¼ cup warm water
- ✓ 1 tablespoon of your favorite spice blend (one without sugar and salt)

DIRECTIONS

1) Preheat the oven to 350°. Line a bread pan with a parchment paper or butter.

2) In a large bowl, stir together dry ingredients. Stir in the eggs and walnut oil, apple cider vinegar, and seasoning. Then the warm water. Dough will look more "wet" than a traditional dough.

3) Transfer the batter to parchment paper lined bread pan.

4) Bake for 45-55 minutes. The bread is done when a toothpick inserted in the center comes out clean, and the top is firm and crust-like.

5) Allow the bread to cool before removing from the pan and slicing.

6) Tip: make several batches and freeze. This will last for 4 months.

OAT FIBER BREAD GLUTEN FREE

Servings	Prep Time	Cook Time
2	5 mins	2 mins

INGREDIENTS

- ✓ ½ cup oat fiber
- ✓ 1 teaspoon of your favorite spice blend (one without sugar and salt)
- ✓ 1/2 teaspoon of unsweetened unflavored gelatin
- ✓ 1 teaspoon aluminum free baking powder
- ✓ 1 teaspoon birch xylitol (powdered)
- ✓ 1 egg
- ✓ 2 tablespoons of sparkling water (room temperature)

DIRECTIONS

1) Butter a 4-cup glass measuring cup. Mix all your ingredients together except the sparkling water for 2 minutes.

2) Now add the sparkling water. Spoon into the measuring cup. Microwave for 120 seconds.

3) Tip: use coffee grinder to powder the birch.

GLUTEN-FREE HAMBURGER BUNS

Servings	Prep Time	Cook Time
12	10 mins	15 mins

Variations: Sesame seeds, Dried onion, Red pepper flakes, Bacon bits, Cheese. Sprinkle any of these choices before placing your batter in your container.

INGREDIENTS

- ✓ ½ cup almond flour
- ✓ ¼ cup coconut flour
- ✓ ¼ cup oat fiber
- ✓ 1 tablespoon of your favorite sugar-free spice blend
- ✓ 1 tablespoon baking powder
- ✓ ½ cup walnut oil
- ✓ ¼ cup sour cream
- ✓ 1 egg
- ✓ 3 tablespoons sparkling water

DIRECTIONS

1) In separate bowl mix almond flour, coconut flour, oat fiber, spice blend and baking powder. Whisk and mix well together. Set aside.

2) In mixer add the oil sour cream and seasoning. Mix for two minutes. Add the egg and half of the dry ingredients. Mix for one minute. Add the rest of the dry ingredients. Mix for one minute. Add the sparkling water last. Mix for 20 seconds.

3) Pour into your hot whoopee pie maker machine or spoon into your oven whoopie pie pan. This recipe can also be done in the microwave. You will need a microwave safe bowl. Place parchment paper in the bowl, enough to come out the top of the bowl.

4) Microwave 60 seconds.

5) Tip: the buns can be cut in half for thin buns.

SPINACH AND FLAX WRAPS GLUTEN FREE

Servings	Prep Time	Cook Time
6	5 mins	30 seconds

INGREDIENTS

- ✓ 10-ounce package frozen chopped spinach (or fresh)
- ✓ 3/4 cup flaxseed meal
- ✓ ¼ cup oat fiber
- ✓ ¼ cup garbanzo bean flour
- ✓ 1egg
- ✓ 1 tablespoon unflavored unsweetened gelatin
- ✓ 1 tablespoon of your favorite sugar-free spice blend
- ✓ 1/2 teaspoon lemon juice (true lemon crystallized lemon)
- ✓ 1 teaspoon baking powder

DIRECTIONS

1) Place all ingredients in a mixer for two minutes.

2) Form into 6 equal balls. Place each ball separately on parchment paper. Add another sheet of parchment paper on top. Flatten with rolling pin until desired size.

3) Microwave for 30 seconds. Store in refrigerator.

4) Variations: add seeds and nuts. Add bacon. Omit the spinach and add ½ cup of favorite hard cheese finely grated.

ULTRA-LOW CARB TORTILLAS

Servings	Prep Time	Cook Time
8	5 mins	10 seconds

I was working on a dumpling recipe and it was a total bust. I was ready to throw the whole thing into the garbage. Then God gave me an idea... Add some corn essence and try to make a tortilla. So, I added the corn essence. I took a piece of parchment paper, spread the dough out and microwaved it for 10 seconds. And wow, it's fantastic! It has the texture and the taste of a corn tortilla. I can see enchiladas, nachos, tacos, tamales and even wraps being made. It's pliable, and tasty.

Variation: Create tortilla chips by sprinkling hot & spicy (without sugar or salt) onto the tortilla before microwaving. Microwave for 10 seconds as if making a tortilla. Remove and cut into triangles and microwave in additional 10 seconds increments until you reach the desired "crunch" level.

INGREDIENTS

- ✓ 2 tablespoon walnut oil
- ✓ ½ cup oat fiber
- ✓ ½ cup almond flour
- ✓ ½ teaspoon salt
- ✓ 1 teaspoon of your favorite spice blend (with no sugar or salt)
- ✓ ¼ teaspoon of corn essence
- ✓ 4 tablespoons bone broth
- ✓ 1 egg

DIRECTIONS

1) Mix all ingredients together in a bowl. On parchment paper, place 1 tablespoon of dough. Place another sheet of parchment paper on top.

2) Spread with a rolling pin, drinking glass, or spatula. Try to spread as thin, and evenly round, as you can. The tortilla should be about 4 inches around. Just make it as even as you can.

3) Keep both sheets of parchment paper on the tortilla and place in the microwave for 10 seconds. Let cool 5 seconds then carefully separate from the parchment.

4) Refrigerate extra tortillas in an airtight container. Microwave for another 10 seconds if the tortilla becomes too soft.

CAULIFLOWER CRUST FOR ANY TYPE OF PIZZA

Servings	Prep Time	Cook Time
6	10 mins	24 mins

You can buy cauliflower crust in the frozen section of most grocery stores. However, the carbs and sugar are higher than if you make it yourself. This means you will likely need to consume smaller portions if using store-bought crusts.

Add your favorite sauce (low sugar of course) and favorite toppings. TIP: Make 2 or more crusts for use later. Store in freezer bags until needed.

INGREDIENTS

- ✓ 1 head of cauliflower (grated or riced to make 3 cups)
- ✓ 8 ounces mozzarella cheese. (finely grated)
- ✓ ¼ cup parmesan cheese finely grated.
- ✓ 1 egg
- ✓ Season to taste with your favorite Italian spice blend (one without sugar and salt)

DIRECTIONS

1) Microwave the grated cauliflower for 2 minutes stir and repeat until tender. Squeeze the moisture out with a cheesecloth or clean dish towel. This is the hardest part of the pizza. Remember the pizza video of the dough spinner pizza man. I would rather squeeze than throw. Yikes!

2) Mix all ingredients together.

3) Pour onto parchment paper cut the size of your pizza stone or baking sheet.

4) Place a second sheet of parchment paper on top and roll out as thin as you like.

5) Pull the top piece of parchment paper off and discard. Place the rolled-out crust in your pan of choice. Bake at 375° for 14 minutes. Yes, that's right bake first.

6) Now the fun part. Bring your pizza crust out of the oven and add your favorite sauce (if desired) and toppings. If you use a pre-made sauce you want it to be thick, so it does not soak your crust and make it soggy. You can add arrow root, or oat fiber or add 1 egg whisked to 8 ounces of sauce to thicken the sauce before it goes on.

7) Bake at 375° for 8 to 10 minutes. Depends on how your top is looking. It may require longer.

   Experiment with any zero sugar or low sugar topping you like. You never know what new combination will tickle your taste buds!

RADISH CRUST WHITE PIZZA – 0 SUGAR, 1 CARB

Servings	Prep Time	Cook Time
6	15 mins	45 mins

Variations: Chicken barbecue, Bacon cheddar, chicken blue cheese, tuna and capers. Because of the texture of the crust no sauce is needed.

INGREDIENTS

Crust:

- ✓ 4 cups radishes
- ✓ 1 tablespoon minced garlic
- ✓ 1 tablespoon of your favorite sugar-free Italian spice blend
- ✓ 2 tablespoons oat fiber
- ✓ 2 eggs
- ✓ 2 tablespoons heavy whipping cream
- ✓ 1cup fine mozzarella cheese
- ✓ ¼ cup fine parmesan cheese

Toppings:
- ✓ 1 ounce sliced thin olives
- ✓ ½ cup Juliane sliced sweet onion
- ✓ 1ounce pork salami
- ✓ 1 cup shredded mozzarella
- ✓ ¼ cup fresh spinach

DIRECTIONS

1) Scrub the radishes and quarter them. Cook them for 4 minutes in the minute pot. Let them cool down. Drain well.

2) Run them through the food processor. Move them to the mixer. Add one cup of finely shredded mozzarella two eggs and heavy whipping cream and the seasoning. Whip for one minute.

3) On a parchment lined pizza stone, spread the radish mixture out (at least ½ inch thick). Bake at 350° for 20 minutes.

4) Bring the crust out and put the toppings over the top of your crust.

5) Bake 375° for 15 to 20 minutes.

DEEP DISH PROSCIUTTO BASIL PIZZA

Servings	Prep Time	Cook Time
6	20 mins	40 mins

INGREDIENTS

Crust:

- ✓ 3 cups finely chopped cauliflower (finer than riced)
- ✓ 2 tablespoons oat fiber
- ✓ 1/2 cup grated parmesan
- ✓ 6 ounces fine mozzarella
- ✓ 2 eggs
- ✓ 1 tablespoon Italian spice

Sauce:

- ✓ 1 teaspoon Italian spice
- ✓ 1 teaspoon garlic powder
- ✓ 1 teaspoon salt
- ✓ ½ teaspoon black pepper
- ✓ ½ cup cream cheese
- ✓ 4 tablespoons Heavy whipping cream

Toppings:
- ✓ 4 ounces Prosciutto (cut in 2-inch strips)
- ✓ ½ cup rough cut red onion
- ✓ 1 cup fresh basil
- ✓ 6 ounces finely grated Mozzarella
- ✓ ½ cup olives (Kalamata or medley)

DIRECTIONS

1) Sauce: mix cream cheese, parmesan, garlic powder and heavy whipping cream.

2) Crust: mix 4 ounces of mozzarella with cauliflower first. Then mix oat fiber, salt, pepper and Italian spice. Add the eggs last.

3) Place parchment paper in a 10-inch deep dish pizza stone or casserole dish or round cake pan. If a cake pan, then one pan will be a deep dish, but you won't have enough dough to make a second deep-dish, so you can make that a thin crust.

4) Pour the dough into the pan of choice. Use a spatula or a spoon to push the dough up the walls of the pan at least 1 inch.

5) Bake at 375° for 15 minutes. Bring out of the oven and add the sauce and toppings.

6) Add the sauce first. Then the meat, onion, olives, basil and mozzarella last.

7) Put back in the oven at 350° for 20-25 minutes.

MASHED CAULIFLOWER TO REPLACE MASHED POTATOES

Cauliflower is low in calories and carbs much lower than Starchy vegetables like potatoes, corn and peas. Cauliflower Can be mashed, chopped, riced. It's a great substitute for rice, potatoes, grits and even macaroni noodles. Starch turns to sugar.

This recipe is easier than mash potatoes. Since cauliflower cooks faster than potatoes. Less prep time, no peeling and healthier for you. Cauliflower doesn't turn to sugar…

INGREDIENTS

- ✓ 1 head of cauliflower
- ✓ 3 tablespoons butter
- ✓ ¼ cup sour cream
- ✓ 1 tablespoon of your favorite spice blend (one without sugar and salt)
- ✓ ½ teaspoon salt

DIRECTIONS

1) Since cauliflower cooks faster than potatoes, steam the cauliflower and then drain it.

2) Using a food processor, blender or potato masher (the food processor makes them the creamiest), add the rest of your ingredients. Mix till creamy.

3) Variations: Bake in the oven at 350° for 15 minutes. Add cheese curry powder chopped bacon herbs rosemary time parsley.

Sides

GRITS BOWL

Servings	Prep Time	Cook Time
4	5 mins	6 mins

Variations: Hot sauce, Gravy, Jelly or cheese spoon on top.

INGREDIENTS

- ✓ 2 cups finely ground cauliflower (see my instructions)
- ✓ ½ cup of water
- ✓ 1 tablespoon of butter
- ✓ ¼ Salt
- ✓ Pepper to taste
- ✓ ½ cube chicken bouillon or beef
- ✓ ½ cup heavy whipping cream or milk
- ✓ 2 scrambled eggs
- ✓ ¼ cup chopped bacon ham sausage

DIRECTIONS

1) In a saucepan place the cauliflower, 1 tablespoon of butter, the bouillon cube, salt and pepper. Sauté for two minutes, stirring constantly.

2) Now add your water and cook for an additional six minutes, stirring so that it doesn't stick. Turn your heat down to simmer at this time.

3) Now add your heavy whipping cream. Cook 1 or 2 minutes depending on the thickness you like. Some people like grits soupier. Then turn the heat off and remove.

4) Scoop onto a plate or bowl. Place two spoons of scrambled eggs in the center of the spooned grits. Sprinkle chopped bacon or ham or sausage. Add any other toppings you would like.

SIMPLE FAKE POTATO SALAD

Servings	Prep Time	Cook Time
6	10 mins	10 mins

Variations: add bacon, add ham, add cheese. You can bake this in the oven for 20 minutes with cheese on top.

INGREDIENTS

- ✓ 10 to 12 Radishes cubed (Black and white if you can find them)
- ✓ ¼ cup chopped onion (red onion is prettier in the salad)
- ✓ 2 hardboiled eggs (separated)
- ✓ 2 small chopped fine dill pickles
- ✓ 2 teaspoons Dijon mustard
- ✓ 2 tablespoons heavy whipping cream
- ✓ 2 tablespoons sour cream (optional)
- ✓ 1 teaspoon salt
- ✓ ½ teaspoon black pepper
- ✓ 2 teaspoons of your favorite spice blend that does not contain sugar or salt

DIRECTIONS

1) Peel and cube radishes, Place radishes in a steamer or microwave to cook. Once soft, pour them into a bowl of ice and water until cooled. Strain them. I like to marinate them in the refrigerator with spices overnight for stronger flavor.

2) Chop your onions, pickles, egg whites into the bowl.

3) In a blender or coffee grinder, put your egg yolks, mustard, heavy whipping cream, sour cream, salt, pepper and your favorite spice blend (that does not contain sugar or salt) until smooth.

4) Mix everything together in the bowl. Garnish with dill or chives.

5) This is a dish that is better after it has been chilled overnight. You can also add cheese and bake this in a casserole dish at 350° for 20 minutes.

GREEN TOMATO CHUTNEY

INGREDIENTS

- ✓ 2 chopped green tomatoes
- ✓ 2 tablespoons olive oil
- ✓ 1 cup chopped onion
- ✓ 1 cup granny smith apple
- ✓ 1 tablespoon of your favorite spice blend that does not contain sugar or salt
- ✓ ½ teaspoon mixed pepper
- ✓ 1 teaspoon salt

DIRECTIONS

1) Mix everything together in a bowl refrigerate.

2) This is great on top of a salad, any meat, you can also put it in a skillet and sauté it as a topping on steak.

BROCCOLI STIR-FRY

Servings	Prep Time	Cook Time
6	5 mins	6-10 mins

Tip: This is a quick stir-fry. Add a salad or an almond flour bread and you have a meal.

INGREDIENTS

- ✓ 1 cup precooked meat (chicken, beef, or pork …)
- ✓ 1 bag frozen broccoli florets
- ✓ ¼ teaspoon salt
- ✓ ¼ teaspoon pepper
- ✓ 1 bouillon cube
- ✓ ½ cup cheese (any cheese will do)
- ✓ Optional: nuts and bacon

DIRECTIONS

1) Stir-fry is just that. Stirring a mix of ingredients into a pan and cooking for a short time.

2) Put all ingredients in the pan. Cook for 6 to 10 minutes, testing the broccoli for doneness. When it's soft.

COLLARD GREENS

Servings	Prep Time	Cook Time
12	10 mins	15 mins

INGREDIENTS

- ✓ 32 ounces of washed chopped collard greens
- ✓ 1 medium onion chopped
- ✓ 1 tablespoon minced garlic
- ✓ 4 strips of bacon
- ✓ 2 tablespoons butter
- ✓ 1 teaspoon salt
- ✓ ½ teaspoon pepper
- ✓ 1.5 tablespoons of your favorite sugar-free hot and spicy seasoning blend
- ✓ 1 tablespoon apple cider vinegar
- ✓ 2 cups of water
- ✓ 2 sugar free beef bouillon cube

DIRECTIONS

1) In skillet, place four strips of bacon and 2 tablespoons of butter. Cook until bacon starts to get crispy.

2) Add handfuls of collards, stirring constantly until they are wilted. Don't worry if it looks like you have more collards than you have room for, they wilt down. Keep stirring so they don't get overcooked. Transfer everything to a crockpot or a stewpot. Add the rest of your ingredients.

3) If you are cooking them in a crockpot, cook 2 to 4 hours on low. If you're cooking them on the stove top simmer for 45 minutes or until soft. Collards are one of those dishes that the longer they sit the better they taste. I like to let them cool down, refrigerate them and rewarm them the next day. If they last that long…

JICAMA (POTATOE) SALAD

INGREDIENTS

- ✓ 1 large jicama, peeled and cubed and boiled
- ✓ ¼ cup cubed onion
- ✓ ¼ cup celery, chopped

Dressing:

- ✓ 1/2 cup heavy whipping cream
- ✓ 3 tbsp apple cider vinegar
- ✓ 1 tbsp fresh dill, chopped
- ✓ 2 tsp lemon juice
- ✓ 2 tsp dried mustard
- ✓ 1 tablespoon of your favorite spice blend that does not contain sugar or salt
- ✓ 1/2 tsp salt
- ✓ Freshly ground pepper, to taste

DIRECTIONS

1) Boil the jicama until tender. Run under water and rinse.

2) In a medium bowl, whisk together the ingredients for the dressing.

3) In a separate large bowl, toss together the jicama, onion, and celery. Mix in the dressing, adding more or less to taste. Top with additional dill if desired.

4) Place in the refrigerator chill for 30 minutes before serving.

AU GRATEN JICAMA

Servings	Prep Time	Cook Time
	2 mins	34 mins

Variations: crumbled pork skins on top. Extra cheese on top.

INGREDIENTS

- ✓ 4 tablespoons butter
- ✓ 1½ cups grated parmesan,
- ✓ 1 cup shredded cheddar cheese
- ✓ 1 tablespoon your favorite spice blend that does not contain sugar or salt
- ✓ 2 teaspoons powdered garlic
- ✓ 1 teaspoon salt
- ✓ ½ teaspoon black pepper
- ✓ 2 cups heavy cream
- ✓ 1 cup chicken broth
- ✓ 1½ pounds jicama sliced 1/16" thick

DIRECTIONS

1) Preheat oven to 400°. Butter a shallow 2-qt. baking dish. Microwave the jicama for 3 minutes.

2) Let cool for 2 minutes and microwave 2 minutes. Add your favorite spice blend, salt and pepper and chicken broth. Mix lightly. Set aside.

3) In a bowl mix melted butter, Parmesan, cheddar, cream.

4) Pour the jicama mix into the baking dish.

5) Pour the cream and cheese on top of the jicama. Use a spatula to mix the liquid some.

6) Bake until cream is thickened, and gratin is bubbling. About 20-30 minutes. Let sit 10 minutes before serving.

SPINACH STUFFED BAKED MUSHROOMS

Servings	Prep Time	Cook Time
4	10 mins	15 mins

INGREDIENTS

- ✓ 4 Portobello mushroom caps
- ✓ 2 tablespoons cream cheese
- ✓ 1/4 teaspoon black pepper
- ✓ 3 cups chopped spinach
- ✓ 1/4 cup grated Parmesan
- ✓ 1 tablespoon of your favorite spice blend that does not contain sugar or salt
- ✓ 1 teaspoon oil (walnut or avocado)

DIRECTIONS

1) Line a baking sheet with foil and oil. Wipe the mushrooms. Use a spoon to gently scrape out the gills.

2) Mix mushroom gills, cream cheese, salt, black pepper, spinach, cheese and spice blend.

3) Fill each mushroom. Broil 8-10 minutes, at 425°.

4) Place back under the broiler for 2-3 minutes, or until filling is golden.

Salads

BAKED CHICKEN SALAD

Servings	Prep Time	Cook Time
1	7 mins	25 mins

Variations: green bean only, add nuts, add more cheese on top, add chilis

INGREDIENTS

- ✓ 2 cups cooked chicken (cubed or shredded)
- ✓ 2 hardboiled eggs
- ✓ ¼ cup celery
- ✓ ¼ cup onion
- ✓ 2 tablespoon walnut oil
- ✓ 2 cups cheese
- ✓ 1 frozen bag mixed vegetables (12 ounce)
- ✓ ½ cup heavy whipping cream
- ✓ ¼ cup bone broth or chicken broth
- ✓ 3 tablespoons cream cheese
- ✓ 2 vegetable bouillon cubes
- ✓ 1 tablespoon poultry spice

DIRECTIONS

1) In a saucepan add walnut oil, onion, celery, pepper and spice. Cook till onions are translucent. Turn it off remove from heat.

2) Place the frozen vegetables into the saucepan and stir. Crush the bouillon cubes and add to the bone broth.

3) Pour over the vegetables, then add the cream, heavy whipping cream, and cheese.

4) Pour into a well-oiled casserole dish. Bake at 350° for 25 minutes.

Entrees (Lunches, Brunches and Dinners)

CAULIFLOWER CRUST BUFFALO CHICKEN BLUE CHEESE PIZZA

Servings	Prep Time	Cook Time
6	10 mins	25 mins

INGREDIENTS

Crust:

- ✓ 8 ounces mozzarella cheese (finely grated)
- ✓ 4 cups grated cauliflower
- ✓ ¼ cup parmesan cheese finely grated.
- ✓ 1 egg
- ✓ 1 tablespoon favorite Italian spice blend

Sauce:

- ✓ ½ cup of heavy whipping cream,
- ✓ 3 tablespoons of cream cheese,
- ✓ 1 egg,
- ✓ 2 tablespoons of your favorite sugar-free Italian spice blend
- ✓ 1/2 a cup of pecorino parmesan cheese. (finely grated)

Toppings:

- ✓ Add 2 cups chopped chicken
- ✓ ¾ cup, celery,
- ✓ ¼ cup sugar free buffalo sauce, (spoon it in spots all over)
- ✓ ¼ cup of sliced onion,
- ✓ ½ cup chunks of blue cheese
- ✓ 1 ½ cups of mozzarella cheese on top.

DIRECTIONS

1) Mix all of the CRUST ingredients together.

2) Microwave the grated cauliflower for 2 minutes stir and repeat until tender. Squeeze the moisture out with a cheesecloth or clean dish towel. This is the hardest part of the pizza. Remember the pizza video of the dough spinner pizza man. I would rather squeeze than throw. Yikes!

3) Pour onto parchment paper cut the size of your pizza stone or baking sheet.

4) Place a second sheet of parchment paper on top and roll out as thin as you like.

5) Pull the top piece of parchment paper off and discard. Place the rolled-out crust in your pan of choice. Bake at 375° for 14 minutes. Yes, that's right bake first.

6) While your crust is baking, make the sauce. Mix together the SAUCE ingredients. Spread on top of your pizza crust when it has finished baking.

7) If you use a pre-made sauce you want it to be thick, so it does not soak your crust and make it soggy. You can add arrow root, or oat fiber or add 1 egg whisked to 8 ounces of sauce to thicken the sauce before it goes on.

8) Add the TOPPINGS and put back in the oven.

9) Bake at 375° for 10 to 15 minutes. Depends on how the top of the pizza is looking. It may require longer.

CHICKEN AND DUMPLINGS WITH EINKORN FLOUR

Servings	Prep Time	Cook Time
8	15 mins	15 mins

This recipe has some Einkorn flour in it. It does not add much sugar but there is gluten.

INGREDIENTS

Stock:

- ✓ 1 teaspoon salt
- ✓ ½ teaspoon pepper
- ✓ 1 tablespoon sugar-free chicken seasoning blend
- ✓ 2 tbsp walnut oil
- ✓ ¾ cup carrots
- ✓ ½ cup celery diced
- ✓ ½ cup onions diced
- ✓ 3 cloves garlic, minced
- ✓ 2 bay leaves
- ✓ 1 Tbsp chicken bouillon
- ✓ 5 cups chicken broth
- ✓ 2 tablespoons butter
- ✓ 2 tablespoons all-purpose einkorn flour
- ✓ 1/2 cup peas, frozen dumplings:

Dumplings:

- ✓ ¼ cup all-purpose einkorn flour
- ✓ ¼ cup oat fiber
- ✓ 2 tsp baking powder
- ✓ 1 tsp favorite table spice
- ✓ 2 tbsp butter
- ✓ ½ cup heavy whipping cream
- ✓ 2 tablespoons sparkling water (sugar free)

DIRECTIONS

1) In a skillet, place the oil and chicken. Brown all sides and add the onion, celery, garlic, salt, pepper and spice blend. Transfer everything to a minute pot, pressure cooker or crock pot.

2) Use the broth to rinse out the skillet. Take 2 tablespoons of the broth and add the flour. Mix with a fork. Pour into the pot and stir.

3) Mix all the dumpling ingredients together and set aside.

4) When the chicken is done and the sauce is bubbling, drop in big spoonsful of the dumpling dough.

ENCHILADAS

Servings	Prep Time	Cook Time
6	20 mins	20 mins

INGREDIENTS

- ✓ 2 lb. pork butt (can use tamale meat recipe)
- ✓ 2 teaspoons salt
- ✓ 2 tablespoons walnut oil
- ✓ 1 ½ cups water
- ✓ 10 ounces wing sauce (any sugar free no MSG will do)
- ✓ 1 onion diced (2 tablespoons dried onion will work)
- ✓ 12 tortilla wraps (see previous recipe)
- ✓ 1 beefsteak tomato (1 cup cubed)
- ✓ 2 tablespoons Franks hot wing sauce

DIRECTIONS

1) In a large skillet, put in the oil and the pork butt. Brown all four sides. Halfway through the browning add the onions. You're not cooking it all the way through yet, you are just browning the outside.

2) Transfer to a minute pot or pressure cooker. Pour 1½ cups of water into the skillet and scrape all the drippings out and into the pressure cooker.

3) Add the hot wing sauce and the salt. Cook over medium heat. When cooking is complete and cooled down, use a fork to pull apart the meat. You can use a potato masher to separate the meat as well.

4) You want to keep the juice with the meat as you pull apart the meat. It will reabsorb the juice. Put the meat inside the tortillas and roll them up.

5) Place in a greased casserole dish and bake for 10 minutes at 350°

6) Purée 1 beefsteak tomato and 2 tablespoons hot wing sauce. Pour this over the enchiladas. Bake 10 minutes.

LOW CARB SPAGHETTI

Servings	Prep Time	Cook Time
6	8 mins	10 mins

INGREDIENTS

- ✓ 1 package of shirataki spaghetti noodles
- ✓ 1/2 jar of low sugar spaghetti sauce
- ✓ ½ lb. ground pork
- ✓ 1/2lb ground beef
- ✓ Onion to your preference
- ✓ Peppers to your preference
- ✓ Garlic to your preference
- ✓ Parmesan cheese to your preference
- ✓ Season to taste with your favorite Italian spice blend (one without sugar and salt)

DIRECTIONS

1) On a cutting board, cut shirataki noodles in half.

2) In a large pot, add 4 ounces of water and boil.

3) Add 1 packages of shirataki noodles and a teaspoon of salt.

4) Allow noodles to simmer for 5 minutes.

5) Strain the noodles again to remove excess water.

6) In large skillet, cook ground pork and beef with spices, garlic, peppers and onion.

7) Add half a jar of spaghetti sauce and stir continuously.

8) Add shirataki noodles into mixture and continue to stir.

9) Add the cheese on top.

HEALTHY FRIED CHICKEN

Servings	Prep Time	Cook Time
8	20 mins	15 mins

Variations: Hot & spicy chicken marinade, or thyme, rosemary and sage, or lemon and pepper spice marinade.

INGREDIENTS

- ✓ 2 lbs. chicken pieces
- ✓ 2 chicken bouillon cubes
- ✓ 1 teaspoon paprika
- ✓ 1/2 cup water
- ✓ 2 teaspoons salt
- ✓ 1 teaspoon pepper
- ✓ ½ cup sour cream
- ✓ ¼ cup heavy whipping cream
- ✓ 1 cup almond flour
- ✓ ½ cup garbanzo bean flour
- ✓ 1 egg
- ✓ 12 ounces coconut oil
- ✓ 1 stick butter
- ✓ 1 tablespoon of your favorite sugar-free chicken spice blend

DIRECTIONS

1) To make the marinade: dissolve the bouillon cubes (can microwave quickly), add water and paprika. Coat your chicken in the water bouillon paprika mix. Place in a gallon size zip lock bag overnight or for at least four hours.

2) Steam the chicken pieces for 10 to 12 minutes. Then marinade the chicken pieces.

3) In a four-cup bowl, mix garbanzo bean flour, almond flour, salt pepper, chicken seasoning blend and set aside.

4) Crack the egg. Whisk it with the heavy whipping cream and sour cream. Add any spice seasoning you prefer here.

5) Dredge the chicken pieces in the egg, sour cream and heavy whipping cream mixture. Then in the flour mixture.

6) Set on a plate to rest. I sometimes double dredge for a thicker coating.

7) I use coconut oil and butter. Place in a deep small pot. You need at least 4 inches deep of oil to cook the chicken pieces in. Use a candy thermometer to keep and eye on your temperature, 350° to 375° is best.

8) Tip: I have a cookie sheet in the oven at 350° to keep my chicken pieces crispy as they come out.

9) Tip: for the most perfect crispy chicken, I steam my chicken pieces for 10 to 15 minutes ahead of the marinade. This keeps my oil from burning quickly because I'm not frying the chicken as long. I'm just frying it enough to get that crispy coating that we all crave. And when my oil cools down I can freeze it and reuse it again.

TAMALE/ ENCHILADA/ TACO MEAT

Servings	Prep Time	Cook Time
12	10 mins	10 mins

INGREDIENTS

- ✓ 2 pounds pork butt roast (any pork will do, if lean pork you will need to add oil or butter)
- ✓ 2 tablespoons walnut oil (any oil will do)
- ✓ 1 medium onion (sliced anyway you like)
- ✓ ¼ cup minced garlic
- ✓ 1 teaspoon salt
- ✓ 1 ½ cup of water
- ✓ 8 ounces of wing sauce (any sugar-free sauce will do)
- ✓ Optional: jalapeno peppers & chilis if you like them really spicy

DIRECTIONS

1) Place 2 tablespoons of oil of your choice in the skillet. Add the pork butt roast and brown it on all four sides. Two minutes on each side.

2) Add the chopped onions to the skillet. Add the minced garlic when browning the last side of the pork butt roast. Turn the heat off.

3) Pour in 1 ½ cup of water. Pour everything in your minute pot, pressure cooker, or crock pot. Make sure you get all the crumbs out of the skillet.

4) Add your wings and sauce and cook. The minute pot should take 10 minutes. The pressure cooker should take six minutes. The crock pot should take four hours.

QUESADILLAS WITH PORK

Servings	Prep Time	Cook Time
5	10 mins	5 mins

INGREDIENTS

- ✓ 10 tortillas (see previous recipe)
- ✓ 1 cup shredded mozzarella cheese
- ✓ 1cup shredded pepper jack cheese
- ✓ 1 cup spicy cooked pork (see previous recipe)
- ✓ ½ cup chopped onion
- ✓ 5 tablespoons sour cream (optional)
- ✓ 2 tablespoons chopped jalapenos (optional)
- ✓ ½ cup spicy salsa (sugar free)

DIRECTIONS

1) In a large bowl, combine the cheeses, cooked pork, onion and salsa. Mix well and divide into five equal portions on a parchment lined baking sheet with sides place tortillas.

2) Fill the tortillas with the mix. Spread out as close to the edges with a spoon.

3) Place a second tortilla on top and press down. Bake at 350° for 15 minutes or until cheese is melted.

4) Top with sour cream and jalapenos.

5) Let cool and pull the parchment out.

PORK FRIED RICE

Servings	Prep Time	Cook Time
8	10 mins	10 mins

INGREDIENTS

- ✓ 4 cups cauliflower
- ✓ 2 cups cooked pork
- ✓ 2 eggs
- ✓ 2 tablespoons walnut oil
- ✓ ¼ cup chopped onion
- ✓ 2 tablespoons minced garlic
- ✓ ½ cup diced carrots
- ✓ ½ cup frozen peas
- ✓ 3 tablespoons gluten-free soy sauce
- ✓ 2 tablespoon of tahini butter (sesame seed butter)
- ✓ ½ teaspoon black pepper
- ✓ ½ teaspoon salt
- ✓ ¼ cup of chopped celery
- ✓ 1 cup of broccoli

DIRECTIONS

1) Mince the cauliflower till it looks like rice. Grate it or use a food processor.

2) In skillet, add the cauliflower, garlic, onion, carrots, celery, walnut oil salt and pepper. Cook until cauliflower is translucent.

3) Add the rest of the vegetables and continue to cook. Add the Tahini butter, soy sauce and pork.

4) Beat the egg, pour into skillet, stir until egg is cooked. Add the green peas last.

5) Variations: Add nuts, sesame seeds, other vegetables, fish, or beef

MEATLOAF

Servings	Prep Time	Cook Time
8	10 mins	30 mins

Variations: top with onion blueberry glaze, BBQ sauce, Marinara sauce

INGREDIENTS

- ✓ 1lb ground beef (lean)
- ✓ 1 lb. ground pork (if lean add 2 tablespoons oil)
- ✓ ½ cup onion (2 tablespoons dried onion can be substituted)
- ✓ ½ cup oat fiber
- ✓ 2 cups steamed chopped fine broccoli
- ✓ 2 tablespoons of your favorite spice blend (no sugar included)
- ✓ ½ teaspoon salt
- ✓ ½ teaspoon pepper
- ✓ 2 tablespoons apple cider vinegar
- ✓ 2 eggs
- ✓ ½ cup heavy whipping cream

DIRECTIONS

1) Put meat, salt, pepper, onion, spices into a mixer. Mix for three minutes.

2) Add the broccoli and mix for 1 minute. Add the oat fiber, Apple cider vinegar and whipping cream. Add the eggs last.

3) Fill 2 loaf pans, or a 12-inch casserole dish. Bake at 400° for 10 minutes.

4) Then adjust the heat to 350° for 20 minutes. Use thermometer to make sure the interior isn't hotter than 160°.

RICE AND CHICKEN

Servings	Prep Time	Cook Time
6	15 mins	8 mins

INGREDIENTS

- ✓ 2 pounds boneless skinless chicken thighs
- ✓ ½ cup water
- ✓ 1 large cauliflower (can use 12 ounces riced cauliflower)
- ✓ 2 teaspoons of your favorite sugar-free chicken flavoring spice blend.
- ✓ 1 tablespoon butter
- ✓ 2 tablespoons fresh sweet onion (can use dried onion)
- ✓ ¼ cup sweet peas (fresh or frozen avoid frozen using sugar for preservation)
- ✓ 1 carrot (no longer than 4 inches, this is more for color than nutrients)
- ✓ ¼ cup heavy whipping cream
- ✓ 1 vegetable bouillon cube (sugar free non-msg)
- ✓ 1 chicken bouillon cube (sugar free non msg)
- ✓ ½ teaspoon black pepper.

DIRECTIONS

1) In a minute pot or pressure cooker, cook boneless skinless chicken thighs and 1 teaspoon of your chicken spice and ½ cup water. Cook for five minutes.

2) While that's cooking, rice your cauliflower in a food processor or with grater. Chop your onions and your carrots.

3) Combine the two bouillon cubes in the butter and heavy cream. You can crush them, or you can microwave slightly to dissolve them.

4) Pull the chicken skin out of the minute pot and save it. You can freeze them to cook latter. They bake in the oven for chicken skin snacks.

5) In the minute pot, add to the chicken the cauliflower, onion carrot, the heavy whipping cream butter, two bouillon cubes mixture and cook for 1 minute. Add the black pepper and the fresh peas. Stir well and serve.

PURÉED RADISH WITH HAM AND SWISS CHEESE BAKE

Servings	Prep Time	Cook Time
4	5 mins	30 mins

INGREDIENTS

- ✓ 2 cups purée radishes
- ✓ 1 cup tiny cubed ham
- ✓ ½ cup of sliced onion
- ✓ ½ teaspoon garlic powder
- ✓ 6 slices Swiss cheese
- ✓ ¼ cup heavy whipping cream
- ✓ ½ teaspoon salt
- ✓ 2 pinches black pepper
- ✓ 1 teaspoon butter
- ✓ 2 eggs

DIRECTIONS

1) Boil peeled radishes until tender.

2) Puree radishes. Mix radish puree, onion powder, garlic powder, salt, pepper, heavy whipping cream and ham and eggs.

3) Butter a 6-cup oven safe glass container, round or square.

4) Spoon the pureed radish mixture into container. Layer the onion on top. Then layer the Swiss cheese on top.

5) Bake at 350 for 20 minutes.

CAULIFLOWER AND HAM BAKE

Servings	Prep Time	Cook Time
6	10 mins	20 mins

Variations: cheese on top, beef tips instead of ham, cracklings with the ham.

INGREDIENTS

- ✓ 3 cups minced cauliflower (food processor is best)
- ✓ 2 cups cubed ham
- ✓ 1 tablespoon walnut oil
- ✓ ¼ cup chopped onions
- ✓ 1 cup chicken broth
- ✓ 1 cup heavy whipping cream
- ✓ 1 tablespoon favorite salt free spice
- ✓ ½ teaspoon black pepper
- ✓ ½ teaspoon cayenne pepper
- ✓ ½ teaspoon corn essence
- ✓ 1 teaspoon unflavored unsweetened gelatin

DIRECTIONS

1) In a skillet, add oil, onion, ham and spices. Cook until onions are translucent.

2) Add chicken broth and cauliflower. Cook until it boils. Turn it off.

3) Add heavy whipping cream, black pepper, cayenne pepper, corn essence and gelatin.

4) Transfer to a greased casserole dish. Bake at 350° for 20 minutes.

SALMON PATTIES

Servings	Prep Time	Cook Time
6	mins	20 mins

Variations: serve over rice cauliflower. Add cheese, serve with radish carrot slaw

INGREDIENTS

- ✓ 1 can of salmon (can use tuna)
- ✓ 4 ounces cream cheese
- ✓ 1 tablespoon favorite fish spice
- ✓ 1 teaspoon lemon juice
- ✓ 2 teaspoons horseradish sauce
- ✓ ½ teaspoon Worcestershire sauce
- ✓ ½ teaspoon black pepper
- ✓ ¼ almond flour (any flour will work)
- ✓ 2 eggs

DIRECTIONS

1) Mix everything together except the salmon. Once it's well mixed, fold in the can of salmon. This is so you can have flakes of the salmon in the patties.

2) Form patties and place on parchment paper lined baking sheet with sides. Bake 350° for 20 minutes.

SAUSAGE KALE JICAMA ONE POT MEAL

Servings	Prep Time	Cook Time
8	10 mins	10 mins

This recipe mimics a soup from a popular Italian restaurant without the starch and sugar.

INGREDIENTS

- ✓ 1 jicama cut into 2-inch pieces
- ✓ 2 tablespoons apple cider vinegar
- ✓ 1 tablespoon Dijon mustard
- ✓ 1 tablespoon favorite all-purpose spice blend
- ✓ 1/4 teaspoon pepper
- ✓ 1/2 cup chopped onion
- ✓ 1 lb. Smoked kielbasa or Polish sausage, cut into 1/4-inch slices
- ✓ 3 cups kale
- ✓ 2 cups beef broth (can use 2 bouillon cubes dissolved in 2 cups of water)

DIRECTIONS

1) Mix all ingredients together in a minute pot, pressure cooker or crockpot.

2) Cook in a minute pot for 5 minutes.

3) If using a pressure cooker, then 4 minutes.

4) If using a crockpot, then 3 hours.

BEEF STEW

Servings	Prep Time	Cook Time
6	10 mins	15 mins

Variations: make with Chicken, add ¼ cup lima beans (this has higher sugar content) but gives it more of a succotash flavor.

INGREDIENTS

- ✓ 2 pounds stew meat
- ✓ 2 tablespoons walnut oil
- ✓ 1 cup of water (may need to add ½ cup later)
- ✓ 1 beefsteak tomato chopped
- ✓ 1 chopped onion
- ✓ ¼ cup celery
- ✓ ½ teaspoon garlic powder
- ✓ 1 tablespoon favorite all-purpose spice blend
- ✓ 2 cups cut cauliflower stalks (they resemble potatoes)
- ✓ 1 chopped carrot
- ✓ 1 teaspoon salt
- ✓ ½ teaspoon black pepper
- ✓ 2 vegetable bouillon cubes
- ✓ 1 cup beef broth
- ✓ ½ cup of sweet peas

DIRECTIONS

1) Chop all vegetables. In a skillet, place the oil and beef. Cook until brown on all sides.

2) Add onion, celery and all the spices. Cook for 2 minutes.

3) Transfer everything to a minute pot, pressure cooker or crock pot. Cook according to the pot.

4) Tip: serve with corn essence muffins or over shirataki rice.

MICROWAVE SHRIMP AND SHIRITAKE RICE CASSEROLE

Servings	Prep Time	Cook Time
8	5 mins	5 mins

Variations; Bake in a casserole at 350° for 20 minutes. Add more kale. Add nuts. Serve with a salad.

INGREDIENTS

- ✓ 1 ½ pounds cooked shrimp
- ✓ 1 lb. Chicken sausage with kale (mild flavor)
- ✓ 2 tablespoons oil
- ✓ ½ cup butter (room temperature)
- ✓ ½ cup cream cheese
- ✓ 1 cup heavy whipping cream
- ✓ 1 cup shredded parmesan cheese (put on last)
- ✓ 2 cups sliced mushrooms
- ✓ ¼ cup green pepper chopped
- ✓ ¼ cup red pepper chopped
- ✓ ¼ cup onion chopped
- ✓ 1 tablespoon favorite spicy blend seasoning
- ✓ 1 teaspoon salt
- ✓ 2 teaspoon Worcestershire sauce
- ✓ 2 cups cooked shirataki rice (this is made from a root and has no carbs or sugar)

DIRECTIONS

1) In a saucepan, add oil, sausage, peppers, onion and dry spices. Cook until sausage is done. Take off the heat and stir in the cooked shrimp.

2) In a separate bowl add softened butter, cream cheese, and heavy whipping cream and Worcestershire sauce. Mix well.

3) Cook the rice separately. Add the cream sauce to the rice. Mix the ingredients together.

4) Butter 4-inch oven safe ramekins or microwaveable bowls. Fill ¾ full. Sprinkle parmesan cheese on top. Microwave for 30 seconds.

CHICKEN AND RICE

Servings	Prep Time	Cook Time
6	10 mins	15 mins

Variations; bake in casserole dish at 350° for 20 minutes for crispiness. Add mixed vegetables and cheese and bake. Serve with a salad.

INGREDIENTS

- ✓ 2 cups cooked chicken
- ✓ 4 cups cooked shirataki rice
- ✓ 1 tablespoon favorite chicken spice blend
- ✓ ½ cup chicken broth
- ✓ 2 tablespoons butter
- ✓ ½ cup cream
- ✓ ½ cup sweet peas

DIRECTIONS

1) Cook the rice according to instructions.

2) Mix cream, butter, spice and chicken broth together in a saucepan.

3) Add the cooked chicken and rice stir well. Add the sweet peas last.

MASHED JICAMA POTATOES RECIPE

Servings	Prep Time	Cook Time
12	10 mins	10 mins

Low in calories but high in a few vital nutrients. Jicama's fiber is laden with oligo fructose inulin, which has zero calories and doesn't metabolize in the body. Mashed jicama can be used as a substitute for mashed potatoes.

- ✓ 2 Jicama peeled and cubed
- ✓ 2 teaspoons salt
- ✓ ½ teaspoon pepper
- ✓ 1 tablespoon minced garlic
- ✓ ½ cup heavy whipping cream
- ✓ 4 tablespoons butter

1) Simply peel the jicama, then cube it and boil it in water, with salt and garlic.

2) Simmer the jicama until it is fork-tender, then drain and mash it with a potato masher.

3) Add butter and milk or cream and stir until the mash is light and fluffy.

RASPBERRY BIRCH CUSTARD KUCHEN

Servings	Prep Time	Cook Time
12	10 mins	30 mins

This recipe uses Einkorn flour, so it's not gluten-free.

INGREDIENTS

- ✓ ½ cup einkorn flour
- ✓ ½ cup coconut flour
- ✓ ¼ cup almond flour
- ✓ ¼ cup oat fiber
- ✓ 1/2 teaspoon salt
- ✓ 1/2 cup cold butter
- ✓ 2 tablespoons heavy whipping cream
- ✓ ½ cup birch xylitol (powdered)
- ✓ 2 teaspoons baking powder

Filling:

- ✓ 3 cups fresh raspberries (or any type of berry)
- ✓ ½ cup birch xylitol (powdered)
- ✓ 1 tablespoon einkorn flour
- ✓ 2 large eggs, beaten
- ✓ 1 cup heavy whipping cream
- ✓ 1 teaspoon vanilla extract

DIRECTIONS

1) In a bowl, combine flours and salt; cut in butter. Combine the birch and remaining ingredients. Pour into the bottom of a greased 13x9" baking dish.

2) Arrange raspberries over crust.

3) In a large bowl, combine birch and flour. Stir in eggs, cream and vanilla; pour over berries.

4) Bake at 375° for 40-45 minutes or until lightly browned. Serve warm or cold. Store in refrigerator.

OVEN FRIED GREEN TOMATOES

Servings	Prep Time	Cook Time
4	10 mins	15 mins

Variations: marinade overnight in Apple cider vinegar and black pepper. Marinade overnight in pureed granny Smith apples and cream.

INGREDIENTS

- ✓ 2 medium green tomatoes (the darker the color the tarter the taste)
- ✓ 1 egg
- ✓ 1 cup oil (any nut oil will do)
- ✓ 3 tablespoons of butter
- ✓ 1 tablespoon favorite spice blend
- ✓ ½ cup heavy whipping cream
- ✓ 3 tablespoons sour cream
- ✓ ½ cup almond flour
- ✓ ½ cup oat fiber
- ✓ 1 teaspoon salt
- ✓ ½ teaspoon black pepper

DIRECTIONS

1) Mix the flour and set aside. In a separate bowl mix the sour cream egg and heavy whipping cream.

2) Slice tomatoes on a plate and sprinkle with salt-and-pepper and seasoning. Refrigerate for an hour.

3) Dredge the tomatoes in the egg, whipping cream mixture. Then dredge in the flour mixture.

4) In a hot skillet, add walnut oil and butter. Cook until crust forms. Place on wire rack with a pan underneath.

5) Sprinkle a little more salt and Pepper and the spice bake at 350° for 20 minutes or until brown.

6) Serve with horseradish sauce

Condiments

RANCH DRESSING

Variation: add blue cheese or feta

INGREDIENTS

- ✓ ½ cup heavy whipping cream
- ✓ ½ cup sour cream
- ✓ 1.5 tablespoons of your favorite spice blend, preferably with a citrus flavor (no sugar added)
- ✓ 1 teaspoon powdered birch xylitol
- ✓ 1 teaspoon apple cider vinegar.

DIRECTIONS

1) Whisk all ingredients together.

2) Place in container and refrigerate.

CREAMY AVOCADO DRESSING

INGREDIENTS

- ✓ 1 avocado or three avocados
- ✓ 3 tablespoons heavy whipping cream
- ✓ ½ teaspoon lemon juice
- ✓ 1 tablespoon of your favorite spice blend (no sugar added)
- ✓ 2 teaspoons apple cider vinegar

DIRECTIONS

1) Purée the avocados in a food processor, coffee grinder or blender.

2) Add the rest of the ingredients as listed and mix well.

3) Put in a container and refrigerate.

RED ONION BLUEBERRY DRESSING / GLAZE

I like to use this on salads, ham, chicken, fish. Less than 2 grams of natural sugar for 4 servings.

INGREDIENTS

- ✓ ½ cup red onions (diced fine)
- ✓ 10 blueberries
- ✓ ¼ teaspoon salt
- ✓ ¼ teaspoon pepper
- ✓ 1 tablespoon walnut oil (olive oil works also)
- ✓ 3 tablespoons heavy whipping cream (water will work as well)

DIRECTIONS

1) In small sauce pan put oil and onions stirring constantly cooking for 3-5 minutes.

2) Add the blueberries stirring constantly, chopping as you go. Add the salt, pepper and cream. Use immersion blender or blender to puree.

3) Tip: Melt in microwave to be pourable.

CREAMY ITALIAN DRESSING / GLAZE

I use this on salads and fish.

INGREDIENTS

- ✓ 3 tablespoons walnut oil
- ✓ ¼ cup extra virgin olive oil
- ✓ ¼ cup white wine vinegar (any no sugar will do)
- ✓ 1 tablespoon of your favorite Italian spice blend (no sugar included)
- ✓ ½ teaspoon salt
- ✓ ¼ teaspoon coarse ground black pepper (red, white and green work too)
- ✓ 3 tablespoons finely ground Parmesan cheese (Romano works too)
- ✓ 2 tablespoons cream cheese
- ✓ 2 tablespoons heavy whipping cream

DIRECTIONS

1) Mix all ingredients together by hand or in a blender.
2) Store in the refrigerator.

PECAN VINAIGRETTE SALAD DRESSING / MARINADE

Variation: use mixed nuts, grated parmesan, red onion instead of pecans and mustard.

Tip: top with pecans toasted in the microwave to crisp up.

INGREDIENTS

- ✓ 2 tablespoons white wine vinegar
- ✓ 1 tablespoon mustard
- ✓ 1 tablespoon apple cider vinegar
- ✓ 2 teaspoons of favorite spice blend
- ✓ 1 teaspoons garlic powder
- ✓ ½ black pepper
- ✓ ½ cup walnut oil
- ✓ ½ cup olive oil
- ✓ Pecans chopped

DIRECTIONS

1) In a blender or coffee grinder place the vinegars, mustard, Salt, Pepper, garlic and spice blend on high.

2) Add the oil until it thickens.

3) Store in the refrigerator.

SPINACH DIP CHILLED OR BAKED

Variation: bake in well-oiled casserole dish at 350° for 25 minutes. Add bacon, ham, blue cheese. Tip: can use radishes or jicama

INGREDIENTS

- ✓ 1 10-ounce package frozen chopped spinach thawed, with water pressed out (or fresh)
- ✓ 4 ounces cream cheese
- ✓ 4 ounces sour cream
- ✓ 2 tablespoons heavy whipping cream
- ✓ 1 8-ounce can of chestnuts chopped
- ✓ ½ cup chopped onion
- ✓ 1 tablespoon favorite spice blend
- ✓ 1 teaspoon black pepper
- ✓ 1 cup shredded parmesan cheese

DIRECTIONS

1) Mix all ingredients together in a bowl. Refrigerate overnight.

HORSERADISH SAUCE

This is great with fried green tomatoes, fish and beef. Variations: grated sharp cheddar cheese, use in wraps, sandwiches, omelet.

INGREDIENTS

- ✓ 3 tablespoons horseradish sauce (no sugar added)
- ✓ 2 tablespoon heavy whipping cream

DIRECTIONS

1) Mix together and store in the refrigerator.

BOURBON BBQ SAUCE

INGREDIENTS

- ✓ ½ teaspoon liquid hickory smoke
- ✓ 1 teaspoon bourbon extract (sugar free)
- ✓ 2 medium pureed tomatoes
- ✓ ¼ cup water
- ✓ 1 teaspoon unsweetened unflavored gelatin
- ✓ ½ tablespoon steak seasoning
- ✓ 1 teaspoons birch xylitol
- ✓ 1teaspoon apple cider vinegar.

DIRECTIONS

1) Put everything except the bourbon extract in a pot. Bring to a boil, stirring constantly.

2) Let it cool down. Use an immersion blender or pour into a blender. Add the bourbon extract last. Pour into container keep in refrigerator.

3) Tip: make a double batch, place in freezer bag with chicken wings. Freeze for up to 6 months.

KETCHUP

INGREDIENTS

- ✓ 4 beefsteak tomatoes
- ✓ 1 teaspoon salt
- ✓ 1 tablespoon of your favorite spice blend (no sugar included)
- ✓ 2 teaspoons birch xylitol (5 grams of sugar all totaled)
- ✓ 1 teaspoon unsweetened unflavored gelatin

DIRECTIONS

1) Chop tomatoes into 1-inch cubes put in sauce pan with water and all the rest of the ingredients.

2) Bring to a boil, stirring constantly. Use immersion blender to purée.

3) Let it cool down and refrigerate.

MAYONNAISE

INGREDIENTS

- ✓ 2 hard-boiled egg yolks (yokes only)
- ✓ ½ teaspoon salt
- ✓ 1 teaspoon sugar-free seasoning blend
- ✓ ½ teaspoon lemon juice (fresh is best)
- ✓ 1 teaspoon apple cider vinegar
- ✓ 2 tablespoons cream cheese
- ✓ ½ cup organic sour cream
- ✓ 4 tablespoons heavy whipping cream.

DIRECTIONS

1) Add all ingredients to a food processor or blender. Mix until lump free. Store in refrigerator.

2) The egg is a thickener. If it thickens too much, add some water to thin it out.

MARINARA SAUCE

INGREDIENTS

- ✓ 4 cubed beefsteak tomatoes
- ✓ 2 tablespoons walnut oil
- ✓ ¼ cup minced garlic
- ✓ 1 teaspoon onion powder
- ✓ 1 teaspoon salt
- ✓ ¼ teaspoon mixed crushed pepper
- ✓ 1 tablespoon of your favorite sugar-free Italian spice blend
- ✓ ¼ cup chopped green bell pepper
- ✓ ¼ teaspoon 100% cocoa powder
- ✓ one teaspoon powdered birch xylitol
- ✓ ½ cup water.

DIRECTIONS

1) In skillet, place the cubed beefsteak tomatoes, walnut oil, minced garlic, onion powder, salt, pepper, green bell pepper and Italian spices. Sauté for five minutes, stirring constantly.

2) In a separate bowl, add the cocoa powder and birch xylitol together.

3) Sprinkle onto the sauté. Add the water. Use an immersion blender to purée the sauce fast. Put in container and refrigerate.

MAPLE SYRUP

INGREDIENTS

- ✓ ½ teaspoon maple extract
- ✓ 1 teaspoon vanilla
- ✓ Pinch of salt
- ✓ 1 teaspoon apple cider vinegar
- ✓ ½ cup powdered birch xylitol
- ✓ ½ cup heavy whipping cream
- ✓ ¼ cup butter.
- ✓ ¼ cup water
- ✓ 1 teaspoon unsweetened gelatin

DIRECTIONS

1) Place water, butter, heavy whipping cream, birch xylitol, salt, apple cider vinegar, in saucepan.

2) Bring to a boil then turn off and remove from heat.

3) Add maple extract, vanilla extract and unsweetened gelatin. Stir constantly. Pour in container and keep refrigerated.

Sherry Peters

SUGAR-FREE JELLY

Variations: Blueberry lemon, Strawberry lemon, Raspberry lemon.

INGREDIENTS

- ✓ 12 ounces frozen or fresh fruit (strawberries, blueberries, whatever you like)
- ✓ 1/4 cup birch xylitol
- ✓ 1 teaspoon vanilla extract
- ✓ ¼ cup heavy whipping cream
- ✓ 1 packet unsweetened unflavored gelatin
- ✓ ½ teaspoon lemon juice (fresh or pasteurized)

DIRECTIONS

1) Heat all ingredients in a saucepan stirring constantly until it boils.

2) Boil for three minutes and turn it off wait five minutes then use an immersion blender to purée you could also use a ninja or food processor once it's cooled down.

3) Pour into containers and keep in the refrigerator it sets in two hours.

136

SUGAR-FREE ORANGE MARMALADE

Orange zest has 0 sugar 0 carbs

Variations: Jalapenos, Lemon, Lime

INGREDIENTS

- ✓ ½ cup sliced or chopped orange zest (use a garlic press to get oils out)
- ✓ ½ cup birch xylitol powdered (organic stevia works)
- ✓ 1 teaspoon orange extract
- ✓ ½ teaspoon vanilla extract
- ✓ 1 cup water
- ✓ 1 packet unsweetened unflavored gelatin
- ✓ ½ teaspoon lemon juice (fresh or pasteurized)

DIRECTIONS

1) Use a garlic press to squeeze the orange zest into a saucepan.

2) Hold the garlic press over the pot and pour the water through it making sure to get all the oils and zest out.

3) Heat water, birch xylitol and orange zest in a saucepan until it boils. Stirring constantly.

4) Boil for three minutes and turn it off. Let cool for five minutes.

5) Stir in the orange and vanilla extract, lemon juice, gelatin.

6) Then use an immersion blender to mix. You could use a ninja or food processor as well. Pour into containers and keep in the refrigerator. It sets in two hours.

Snacks

HOT WINGS - 0 SUGAR, 0 CARB

Servings	Prep Time	Cook Time
4	5 mins	30 mins

Tip: Reuse the leftover bag of sauce by freezing it until needed. Do not seal tight. It could build up and explode.

INGREDIENTS

- ✓ 12 chicken wings fresh or frozen
- ✓ 2 teaspoon baking soda
- ✓ 2 cups hot wings sauce (or any 0 sugar, 0 carb sauce)
- ✓ Season to taste with your favorite sugar-free, hot and spicy spice blend

INGREDIENTS

1) Rinse chicken wings thoroughly put them in a gallon size Ziploc bag

2) Add all ingredients to the bag. Mix inside the bag until all are coated. You can freeze the entire bag to used later or refrigerate and marinate for up to six hours.

3) Place on rack in a glass casserole dish or baking pan bake at 400° for 15 minutes then reduce the heat to 350°. Bake 15 more minutes or until the outer crust is dark.

4) Tip: baking soda is alkaline, so it raises the PH level of the chicken skin. This breaks down the peptide bonds in the chicken skin to make it crispy.

5) Tip: If you don't have an oven rack to fit in your pan, you can crumble aluminum foil and poke holes through it to raise your wings up.

CHICKEN SKIN BLACK PEPPER SEA SALT CHIPS – 0 SUGAR, 0 CARB

Servings	Prep Time	Cook Time
4	10 mins	25 mins

These can be quite pricey in the stores but cheap and easy to make at home.

Tip: If frozen let thaw out in the refrigerator and pat dry before baking

INGREDIENTS

- ✓ 2 cups cooked chicken skin
- ✓ 1 teaspoon coarse sea salt
- ✓ 1 teaspoon coarse ground black pepper
- ✓ 2 tablespoons Avocado oil (any 0-carb oil will do)
- ✓ Optional: 1 teaspoon barbecue or hot sauce

DIRECTIONS

1) Ready a baking pan with sides, wire rack that fits inside of baking pan. If you've don't have a wire rack in a baking pan you can crumble aluminum foil too lay your chicken skin on.

2) In a bowl, add 2 tablespoons of olive oil, black pepper and sea salt. Mix well.

3) Add one piece of chicken skin at a time into the bowl. Dredge your chicken skin in the olive oil black pepper mix. Be careful during this process that you don't tear the chicken pieces. You want them to stay as large as possible.

4) Lay them on the rack and bake at 375° for 15 to 25 minutes depending on the crispness and the color.

PORK SKIN NACHOS (MICROWAVE OR OVEN) 0 SUGAR, 0 CARB

Servings	Prep Time	Cook Time
4	10 mins	1 min

Tip: These freeze well.

INGREDIENTS

- ✓ 2 cups baked pork skins
- ✓ ½ cup grated jalapeno cheese or any spicy cheese
- ✓ 1-pound ground meat (optional)
- ✓ ¼ cup chopped onions
- ✓ 1 jalapeno (chopped fine)
- ✓ ¼ cup low sugar salsa
- ✓ ¼ sour cream
- ✓ ¼ cup green Verde sauce (or sauce of your choosing)

DIRECTIONS

1) Brown the beef with the Verde sauce until cooked. Set-aside.

2) Microwave baked pork skins for 15 to 20 seconds this makes them crispier so that the moist meat, salsa and cheese do not cause them to disintegrate in your hand.

3) Load your pork skins with meat cheese salsa and enjoy. You can always re-warm in the microwave to get them crispy again.

4) If using the oven, place pork skin nachos on a parchment-lined cookie sheet.

5) Cover with aluminum and bake for 10 minutes at 350° or until cheese is melted

6) The reason for covering the pork skins is they will burn. You want a dry heat.

MICROWAVE CHEESE CHIPS

Servings	Prep Time	Cook Time
2	1 min	1 min

Variations: Pepper jack cheese with crushed peanuts, parmesan and dark chocolate chips,

INGREDIENTS

- ✓ Two 2-inch squares of cheddar cheese
- ✓ 1 tablespoon bacon crumbs
- ✓ 4-inch piece of parchment paper

DIRECTIONS

1) On a microwave safe plate lined with parchment paper place cheese square in the center. Microwave for 20 seconds.

2) Pour off the liquid. Sprinkle the bacon crumbs on top. Microwave 25 more seconds until crisp.

3) Use a flat spatula or butter knife to lift off the plate immediately. Let cool

4) Tip: Microwave temperatures vary. You may need to adjust your cook time a few more seconds.

CHEESE CHIPS WITH CHIA SEEDS

Servings	Prep Time	Cook Time
1	2 mins	1 min

INGREDIENTS

- ✓ 1-inch cheese cube
- ✓ 2 tablespoons of chia seeds

DIRECTIONS

1) Put the cheese cube in the center of a small plate. Microwave for 45 seconds

2) Pour off the liquid fat. Sprinkle the chia seeds immediately. Use a spatula to pull the chip off the plate before it sticks.

STRAWBERRY CREAM SPREAD

Servings	Prep Time	Cook Time
6	3 mins	1 mins

Variations: This makes a great spread for breakfast or as a snack on flax seed crackers.

INGREDIENTS

- ✓ 1 cup chopped fine strawberries
- ✓ 6 ounces cream cheese
- ✓ 1/2 cup of heavy whipping cream
- ✓ 2 tablespoons birch xylitol powdered (swerve or erythritol)
- ✓ 1 teaspoon vanilla extract

DIRECTIONS

1) In a mixer or blender mix the cream cheese, birch, vanilla and the heavy whipping cream for two minutes. Add the strawberries mix until incorporated.

2) Store in refrigerator.

MICROWAVE FLAXSEED CRACKERS

Servings	Prep Time	Cook Time
6	5 mins	1 min

Variations: add parmesan cheese, dried basil, chia seeds

INGREDIENTS

- ✓ 1/3 cup flaxseed meal
- ✓ 1/3 cup oat fiber
- ✓ 2 tablespoons walnut oil
- ✓ 1 teaspoon unsweetened unflavored gelatin
- ✓ 1 teaspoon salt
- ✓ 1 tablespoon favorite Italian spice blend
- ✓ 1 egg
- ✓ 1 teaspoon baking powder

DIRECTIONS

1) Place all ingredients in a mixer. Mix for two minutes.

2) Form into 1-inch balls place on parchment paper. Flatten with rolling pin or tortilla press.

3) Microwave for 20 seconds. If you want them crunchier put them in for 10 seconds more. Store in refrigerator.

SALTED CARAMEL PECANS

Servings	Prep Time	Cook Time
4	5 mins	5 mins

Variations: add cinnamon and nutmeg, add red pepper flakes, add chocolate chips(unsweetened)

INGREDIENTS

- ✓ 2 cups pecan halves
- ✓ ¼ cup birch xylitol
- ✓ 2 tablespoons butter
- ✓ ¼ teaspoon vanilla
- ✓ ¼ teaspoon Sea salt (flakes or coarse)
- ✓ 1 tablespoon Heavy whipping cream

DIRECTIONS

1) In a non-stick skillet or saucepan add butter and pecans. Cook while stirring constantly for 2 minutes.

2) Then add the birch. Continue to stir. Watch the color of the butter. If it starts to get to dark (light color caramel is the color you want), you may need to lower your heat or remove the pan from heat.

3) When the sauce changes color, around 5 minutes, remove from heat. Add the vanilla and heavy whipping cream. Pour into a pan lined with parchment paper.

4) Sprinkle the salt flakes on top and freeze for 2 hours.

SUGAR-FREE DONUT HOLES

Servings	Prep Time	Cook Time
36	5 mins	10 mins

INGREDIENTS

- ✓ 1 stick of organic butter
- ✓ 1/4 cup walnut oil
- ✓ 3 tablespoons sour cream
- ✓ 1/2 cup birch xylitol powdered
- ✓ 1tsp vanilla
- ✓ 1 cup superfine almond flour
- ✓ 1/2 cup coconut flour
- ✓ 2 tsp non-aluminum baking powder
- ✓ 2 eggs (do not over mix)
- ✓ 1/4 cup sparkling water

DIRECTIONS

1) In a large mixing bowl, mix the butter, walnut oil, sour cream, powdered birch and vanilla.

2) Mix together till fluffy, about 3-5 minutes. Set aside for a moment.

3) In a separate bowl, combine the almond flour, coconut flour, and baking powder.

4) Wisk well for 1 minute.

5) Combine both bowls and mix for 1 minute.

6) Incorporate the eggs (one egg at a time) and sparkling water into the mix and mix for another minute. All ingredients should be combined at this time.

7) Add your first batch to the Cake Pop Maker following the directions on the next page. Refrigerate the unused portion while working on your first batch.

CAKE POP MAKER DIRECTIONS

These directions will vary from traditional Cake Pop Maker directions since you are not using traditional flours. Alternative flours cook differently and rise, if at all, differently than traditional flours.

Times may vary based upon the recipe. If so, this will be noted within the specific recipe.

1. Preheat the Cake Pop Maker for 1 minute.

2. Unplug the Cake Pop Maker while you spoon the batter in. Fill each cavity completely but try not to overfill, a little overfill is ok. Cleanup is easy since your surfaces are non-stick.

3. Once all cavities are filled, close the lid and plug back in.

4. Set a timer for 30 seconds. This will give the base of your donut holes time to set.

5. When the timer sounds, using heat gloves, or some form of kitchen mitts or towels, flip the Cake Pop Maker over so the top is now on the bottom and resting on your counter. Use a towel or oven mitt to rest the Cake Pop Maker on if your counters are not heat resistant.

6. Set a timer for 90 seconds.

7. When the timer sounds, flip the Cake Pop Maker back to its normal state and unplug.

8. Set a timer for 2 minutes.

9. When the timer sounds, lift the cake pop maker lid and check the color. Color should be medium to dark brown. If ok, leave the lid open and allow to cool. UNPLUG the Cake Pop Maker while cooling.

10. If additional cooking is desired, close the lid and flip the Cake Pop Maker every 2 minutes, checking for color each time you flip the Cake Pop Maker. Remember to plug the Cake Pop Maker back in to your outlet.

11. If making more donut holes, allow the Cake Pop Maker to cool 2 minutes before removing the donut holes. Then repeat the process beginning at step 1.

12. Enjoy the donut holes as-is, or add powder or other toppings as desired

Powdered Birch:

Take 4 tablespoons of birch xylitol and grind in a coffee grinder to make powder. Remove and place in a small container or bowl. Roll your donut holes in the powder and enjoy!

Refrigerate, or freeze, any left-over powder.

Variations abound…

You could add blueberries, dark chocolate chips, espresso powder or nuts to batter once it is spooned into the cake pop maker.

You could add cinnamon, powdered Chocolate, powdered espresso, powdered peanut flour, to the birch before rolling the donut holes in it...

MICROWAVABLE SINGLE SERVE BROWNIE

Servings	Prep Time	Cook Time
2	5 mins	1.5 mins

INGREDIENTS

Brownie:

- ✓ 2 ounces dark chocolate
- ✓ 2 tablespoons butter
- ✓ 1 tablespoon cream cheese
- ✓ 2 tablespoons birch sweetener
- ✓ ½ teaspoon of vanilla
- ✓ 3 tablespoons coconut flour
- ✓ 2 tablespoons of almond flour (finely ground)
- ✓ 1 tablespoon baking powder
- ✓ 1 egg
- ✓ 1 tablespoon sparkling water
- ✓ Optional: 1 tablespoon chopped nuts or raspberries for a topping

Icing:

- ✓ ½ tablespoon butter
- ✓ ½ tablespoon cream cheese
- ✓ 1ounce dark chocolate
- ✓ 1 tablespoon heavy whipping cream
- ✓ ½ tablespoon Birch xylitol (powdered)

DIRECTIONS

1) Whisk everything together. Butter a 2-cup glass measuring cup.

2) pour the mixture in microwave for 90 seconds. Wait 30 seconds and flip it out onto a plate.

3) Melt the chocolate and the heavy whipping cream for 20 seconds in the microwave.

4) Now whisk in the butter and cream cheese in with the powdered xylitol. Then spread over the brownie.

MICROWAVABLE BANANA NUT CAKE

Servings	Prep Time	Cook Time
8	5 mins	1.5 mins

INGREDIENTS

Banana Nut Cake:

- ✓ ½ cup coconut flour
- ✓ ½ cup oat fiber
- ✓ ½ cup green banana flour
- ✓ ½ cup almond flour
- ✓ ½ cup birch xylitol
- ✓ 1 package gelatin unflavored unsweetened
- ✓ 1 tablespoon baking powder
- ✓ 4 tablespoons butter
- ✓ 2 tablespoons walnut oil
- ✓ ¼ cup heavy whipping cream
- ✓ 3 tablespoons sour cream
- ✓ 2 tablespoons cream cheese
- ✓ 1 ½ teaspoon banana extract
- ✓ ½ teaspoon vanilla extract
- ✓ 2 eggs
- ✓ ½ cup chopped nuts (optional)
- ✓ ¼ cup sparkling water

Icing:

- ✓ 3 tablespoons heavy whipping cream
- ✓ 3 tablespoons cream cheese
- ✓ 2 tablespoons butter
- ✓ ½ cup birch xylitol powdered or swerve
- ✓ ¾ teaspoon banana extract
- ✓ ¼ cup chopped nuts on top
- ✓ 1 tablespoon baking powder

DIRECTIONS

1) Preheat oven to 350°. If microwaving, cut parchment paper to fit into microwavable containers. 4-inch ceramic loaf pans are easiest for the microwave. Metal or glass loaf pans are best for the oven.

2) In a separate bowl: mix coconut flour, oat fiber, banana flour, almond flour, unflavored gelatin, baking powder whisk together.

3) In mixer: combine butter, Walnut oil, birch xylitol, Banana extract, vanilla extract, sour cream, cream cheese and heavy whipping cream mix for two minutes. Add one egg at a time. Mixing for half a minute in between. Add half the flour mixture to the wet mixture. Mix for one minute. Add the rest of the dry ingredients mix well. Add the sparkling water last.

4) If adding nuts: Place them in the bottom of your loaf pan. Spoon in your batter bake at 350° for 15 minutes or until top is not soft. Take out immediately.

5) If microwaving: microwave for 110 seconds on high. Wait 20 seconds lift the parchment paper out of the ceramic loaf pan.

6) To make the icing put all your ingredients in a food processor or hand mixer. Mix until smooth. Spread the icing on top of your cake. Sprinkle chopped nuts on top.

7) Tip: if your microwave over cooks your cake you can spoon heavy whipping cream over the bottom, and it will soften it.

MICROWAVE VANILLA CAKE WITH CHOCOLATE GANACHE

Servings	Prep Time	Cook Time
2	5 mins	1.5 mins

You can push 5 blueberries, raspberries, nuts, chocolate chips, into the cake mix before you microwave.

INGREDIENTS

- ✓ 2 tablespoons of butter
- ✓ 4 tablespoons of coconut flour
- ✓ 2 tablespoons of birch xylitol powdered
- ✓ ½ teaspoon vanilla
- ✓ ½ tablespoon of baking powder (aluminum free)
- ✓ 2 tablespoons of sparkling water.
- ✓ 1 egg

DIRECTIONS

1) Mix all ingredients together. Butter a 2-cup glass measuring cup or line with parchment paper. Spoon the mixture inside.

2) Microwave on high for 90 seconds.

3) Wait 30 seconds and flip it out onto a plate to cool.

Ganache:

- ✓ 1 ounce of dark chocolate, (92% chocolate candy bar)
- ✓ 2 tablespoons of heavy whipping cream.

1) Melt for 20 seconds whisk quickly then pour over the top of cake.

Desserts

CHOCOLATE CHIP COOKIE

Servings	Prep Time	Cook Time
14	5 mins	10 mins

INGREDIENTS

- ✓ 2 eggs
- ✓ ¾ stick of butter
- ✓ ¼ cup of walnut oil
- ✓ 1 teaspoon vanilla
- ✓ ½ cup of birch xylitol
- ✓ 1 ¾ cup almond flour
- ✓ ½ cup oat fiber
- ✓ 3 tablespoons unsweetened gelatin
- ✓ ½ teaspoon baking soda
- ✓ 1 tablespoon aluminum free baking powder
- ✓ 4 ounces sugar free chocolate chips

DIRECTIONS

1) Start oven at 350°

2) Mix almond flour oat fiber gelatin baking soda baking powder together and set aside.

3) Mix the butter and oil vanilla and birch xylitol in a mixer until fluffy. Two minutes.

4) Add one egg at a time mixing for six to 8 turns in between the eggs.

5) Add half of the dry mixture to the wet mixture. Continue mixing for one minute.

6) Add the other half of the dry mixture mix for an additional minute.

7) Add the chips thoroughly mix together.

8) Use a small ice cream scoop, melon baller or spoon to scoop onto parchment paper.

9) Bake at 350 degrees for 10 minutes. Pull out of the oven slide the parchment paper with the cookies onto a cool counter. Let cool 10 minutes. Store in the refrigerator.

PEANUT BUTTER COOKIE

Servings	Prep Time	Cook Time
12	10 mins	10 mins

Variations: chopped peanuts, chocolate chips,

INGREDIENTS

- ✓ ½ cup peanut butter (no sugar added)
- ✓ 2 tablespoons cream cheese
- ✓ 2 tablespoons butter
- ✓ ½ cup birch xylitol powdered
- ✓ 1 teaspoon vanilla extract
- ✓ 1 egg
- ✓ ½ cup coconut flour
- ✓ ½ cup peanut flour
- ✓ ¼ cup oat fiber
- ✓ 1 tablespoon baking powder (aluminum free)
- ✓ 2 teaspoons unsweetened unflavored gelatin
- ✓ 2 tablespoons sparkling water

DIRECTIONS

1) Add peanut butter, cream cheese, butter, birch, vanilla. Mix two minutes with mixer or in a KitchenAid.

2) In separate bowl combine coconut flour, peanut flour, oat fiber, baking powder, and unflavored gelatin. Whisk well.

3) Add eggs. Add half the dry ingredients mixing for one minute add the other half of the dry ingredients mix another minute. Add the sparkling water last.

4) Using small ice cream scoop. Scoop and place on parchment lined baking sheet.

5) Bake at 350° for 10 minutes.

MICROWAVE BUTTER MINTS

Servings	Prep Time	Cook Time
12	5 mins	1 min

INGREDIENTS

- ✓ 1/2 cup of butter (1 stick) at room temperature
- ✓ 1 tablespoon unsweetened unflavored gelatin
- ✓ 4 tablespoons heavy whipping cream
- ✓ 1 cup erythritol or powdered birch or swerve
- ✓ 1 teaspoon crème de menthe preferably, but any mint extract will work
- ✓ 1 pinch of salt (flake or course)
- ✓ 2 drops food coloring (optional)

DIRECTIONS

1) In a glass microwave safe cup, warm heavy whipping cream for 20 seconds.

2) Whisk in the gelatin until dissolved. Add all ingredients to a blender and mix well spoon into a buttered dish r parchment paper shape as desired.

3) Place in freezer for 20 minutes until firm then keep in an airtight container, or in the refrigerator. Can freeze for up to six months.

GARBANZO BEAN FLOUR CHOCOLATE CHIP COOKIES

Servings	Prep Time	Cook Time
12	5 mins	10 mins

INGREDIENTS

- ✓ ½ cup butter
- ✓ ½ cup birch xylitol
- ✓ 1 teaspoon vanilla
- ✓ 1 cup of garbanzo bean flour
- ✓ ½ cup oat fiber
- ✓ ½ tablespoon of baking powder aluminum free
- ✓ 3 ounces of dark chocolate coarsely chopped
- ✓ 1 egg

DIRECTIONS

1) Preheat oven to 350°

2) In a separate bowl, mix Garbanzo bean flour, oat fiber, baking powder.

3) Mix butter, birch, vanilla, for 2 minutes. Add the egg mix well.

4) Add the dry ingredients to the wet. Mix well. Add the chocolate last.

5) Spoon onto parchment paper lined cookie sheet. Bake for 10 to 12 minutes

BUTTER COOKIES

Servings	Prep Time	Cook Time
12	10 mins	10 mins

Variations: 1-inch square of dark chocolate with 1/2 teaspoon heavy whipping cream melted and drizzled over cookies.

INGREDIENTS

- ✓ 1 stick of butter (room temperature)
- ✓ 1/3 cup walnut oil
- ✓ ½ cup powdered birch xylitol
- ✓ 1 teaspoon vanilla
- ✓ ½ teaspoon almond extract
- ✓ ¾ cup almond flour
- ✓ 4 tablespoons coconut flour
- ✓ 3 teaspoons baking powder (aluminum free)

DIRECTIONS

1) Mix butter, oil, birch, vanilla extract and almond extract with hand mixer or KitchenAid for 2 minutes.

2) In separate bowl mix almond flour, coconut flour and baking powder whisk it well.

3) Combine the dry ingredients with the wet ingredients. Mix well.

4) Shape into 1 ½ inch balls and place on parchment lined cookie sheet.

5) Bake at 350° for 10 minutes.

COCONUT FLOUR "SUGAR" COOKIES

Servings	Prep Time	Cook Time
12	5 mins	10 mins

Variations: Unsweetened shredded coconut Mini chocolate chips Chopped raspberries Nuts

INGREDIENTS

- ✓ 1 ¾ cup coconut flour
- ✓ 1 tablespoon aluminum free baking powder
- ✓ 5 tablespoons of butter
- ✓ 1/4 cup coconut oil
- ✓ ½ cup birch xylitol
- ✓ 3 eggs
- ✓ 1 teaspoon vanilla extract
- ✓ 2 tablespoon sparkling water

DIRECTIONS

1) Mix the dry ingredients together in a separate bowl and set aside.

2) Add wet ingredients (except the sparkling water) to a mixer and mix for two minutes.

3) Add the dry ingredients. Mix two minutes. Now add the sparkling water. Just until its mixed. The mixture should be thick. Scoop the dough onto a parchment paper cookie

4) Sheet or silicone mat. Bake at 375° for eight to 10 minutes or when the edges Start looking brown.

CHEWY CHOCOLATE CHIP COOKIES

Servings	Prep Time	Cook Time
18	10 mins	10 mins

Variations: coco powder, Chopped Nuts

INGREDIENTS

Wet ingredients:
- ✓ 1 stick butter
- ✓ ¼ cup walnut oil
- ✓ ½ cup powdered birch xylitol
- ✓ 2 teaspoons vanilla extract
- ✓ ¼ cup sour cream
- ✓ 2 eggs one at a time

Dry ingredients:
- ✓ 1 ½ cup almond flour
- ✓ ½ cup coconut flour
- ✓ ½ cup oat fiber
- ✓ 1 pouch (.25oz) unsweetened unflavored gelatin powder
- ✓ ½ tsp baking soda
- ✓ 2 teaspoons aluminum free baking powder

DIRECTIONS

1) Turn your oven on 350°

2) Mix all wet ingredients for 2 minutes until fluffy (kitchen aide or handheld mixer)

3) Put dry ingredients in a bowl and whisk well before adding to the wet mixture.

4) If the mixture is stiff you can add up to 2 tablespoons of a sparkling water

5) Lastly add 4 ounces of dark chocolate chips. You could make your own chips by crushing a 92% cocoa candy bars.

6) Using small ice cream scoop or large tablespoon

7) Scoop onto parchment papered cookie sheet

8) Bake at 350° for 10 to 12 minutes

PEANUT BUTTER FUDGE

Servings	Prep Time	Cook Time
10	10 mins	5 mins

INGREDIENTS

- ✓ 4 oz dark chocolate chips (sugar free)
- ✓ 1 cup birch xylitol powdered
- ✓ 1 tsp vanilla extract
- ✓ 1 tablespoon butter
- ✓ ¼ cup heavy whipping cream
- ✓ 4 tablespoon cream cheese
- ✓ ¾ cup peanut flour
- ✓ ¼ peanuts

DIRECTIONS

1) Melt the chocolate

2) Add heavy whipping cream and birch in saucepan. Stir constantly for 3 minutes over medium heat.

3) Remove from heat let cool for 3 minutes.

4) Put cream cheese, vanilla, powdered peanut flour in the mixer.

5) Pour the cooled down mixture into the mixer. Hand mixer or kitchen aid. Mix until glossy.

6) If mixture is too runny add some powdered birch. (no more than ¼ cup)

7) Pour into buttered or parchment lined glass container. (I use a square one.)

8) You can add nuts before you pour or after

9) Put in the freezer for 1 hour then transfer to refrigerator.

BLUEBERRY CAKE WITH ICING

Servings	Prep Time	Cook Time
8	10 mins	25-30 mins

2 grams of sugars

INGREDIENTS

Cake:
- ✓ ½ cup almond flour (super fine)
- ✓ ½ cup coconut flour
- ✓ ¼ cup oat fiber
- ✓ 1 tablespoon baking powder (aluminum free)
- ✓ 1 tablespoon unflavored gelatin
- ✓ 4 tablespoons butter (room temperature)
- ✓ ¼ cup walnut oil
- ✓ ¼ cup birch xylitol powdered
- ✓ 2 large eggs
- ✓ 1 teaspoon vanilla extract
- ✓ ¼ cup sour cream
- ✓ 1 cup blueberries

Icing:
- ✓ 1cup cream cheese
- ✓ 2 tablespoons butter
- ✓ 2 tablespoons heavy whipping cream
- ✓ 3 tablespoons birch xylitol (powdered)
- ✓ 10 blueberries for topping

DIRECTIONS

1) Preheat oven to 350°. Put parchment paper in a 9-inch round cake pan. Put the oil, birch, butter, gelatin and vanilla into a bowl and beat until light in color. Add the sour cream and the eggs. Add the flours and baking powder. Mix well. Stir in blueberries. Being gentle to not break the skins on the blueberries.

2) Pour into the prepared pan and bake for 25-30 minutes. The center should feel firm to the touch and spring back when you press it.

3) While the cake is baking, make the icing: Whip the cheese, butter, heavy whipping cream and birch in a bowl until smooth and creamy. When the cake is cooled spread the icing and top with blueberries.

4) Variations: Raspberry, Strawberry, Cinnamon and green apple.

PECAN FUDGE

Servings	Prep Time	Cook Time
8	10 mins	10 mins

INGREDIENTS

- ✓ 4 oz chocolate chips
- ✓ 1 cup birch xylitol powdered or swerve
- ✓ 1 tsp vanilla extract
- ✓ 1 tablespoon butter
- ✓ ¼ cup heavy whipping cream
- ✓ 4 tablespoon cream cheese
- ✓ ½ cup pecans

DIRECTIONS

1) Melt the chocolate

2) Heavy whipping cream and birch in saucepan stir constantly for 3 minutes over med heat.

3) Remove from heat let cool for 3 minutes.

4) Put cream cheese, vanilla, powdered peanut flour in the mixer.

5) Pour the cooled down mixture into the mixer. Mix until glossy.

6) If mixture is too runny add some powdered birch. (no more than ¼ cup)

7) Pour into buttered or parchment lined glass container. (I use a square one.)

8) You can add nuts before you pour or after…

9) Put in the freezer for 1 hour then transfer to refrigerator.

CHEESECAKE 0 CARB 0 SUGAR

Servings	Prep Time	Cook Time
8	10 mins	50 mins

INGREDIENTS

Crust:

- ✓ 1 1/2 cups almond flour
- ✓ ¼ cup oat fiber
- ✓ 1/2 cup butter, melted
- ✓ 1/4 cup birch (powdered)

Filling:

- ✓ 4 packages (8 ounces each) cream cheese, softened
- ✓ ½ cup sour cream
- ✓ 3 tablespoons heavy whipping cream
- ✓ 3/4 cups Birch Xylitol (powdered)
- ✓ 3 tablespoons vanilla extract
- ✓ 1/8 teaspoon salt
- ✓ 4 large eggs, lightly beaten

DIRECTIONS

1) Preheat oven to 325°. Mix flours, butter and birch; press onto bottom and 1-inch up sides of a greased and parchment paper 9-in. Springform pan.

2) In a large bowl, beat cream cheese, birch, sour cream, heavy whipping cream and vanilla and salt until smooth. Add eggs; beat on low speed until well blended. Pour into crust. Place on a baking sheet.

3) Bake until center is almost set, 50-60 minutes. Cool on a wire rack 10 minutes. Loosen sides from pan with a knife. Cool 1 hour longer. Refrigerate overnight, covering when completely cooled.

4) Variations: add chocolate chips, add mint extract to the batter. Add raspberries, blueberries, strawberry or chocolate ganache.

FUDGE WITH WALNUTS

Servings	Prep Time	Cook Time
12	10 mins	1 min

INGREDIENTS

- ✓ 1/2 cup butter, at room temperature
- ✓ 1 (8 ounce) package cream cheese, at room temperature
- ✓ 6 tablespoons unsweetened cocoa powder
- ✓ 1/3 cup chopped walnuts
- ✓ 1/4 cup birch xylitol powdered or swerve
- ✓ 2 tablespoons heavy cream
- ✓ 2 teaspoons vanilla extract

DIRECTIONS

1) Beat butter and cream cheese together in a large microwave-safe bowl using an electric mixer until smooth. Add cocoa powder, walnuts, sugar substitute, heavy cream, vanilla extract. Stir fudge mixture slowly until well combined.

2) Microwave the fudge mixture on high, about 30 seconds. Continue blending with an electric mixer until smooth.

3) Grease a 9 x13 baking pan; spread mixture into the pan in 1 smooth layer. Cover with plastic wrap and refrigerate until set, at least 2 hours. Cut into bars.

About the Author

Sherry Peters was born and raised in the South and enjoyed all the wonders of Southern Cooking throughout her life. After trying to lose weight for years, even decades, she realized she had an addiction. This addiction was literally killing her!

Sherry's addiction was to something that we are all addicted to, some more than others. This addiction is so widespread throughout our country and even the world. In fact, the WHO already calls this a global epidemic.

Sherry's addiction was to SUGAR! Sugar was everywhere in her diet, whether at home or at work. Sherry declared war on sugar and realized she had to be totally *gone with the sugar* if she was going to be around to enjoy life with her husband, her children and her grandkids.

Sherry lost 106 pounds over 7 months and has maintained this weight loss for over one year! She did so by developing a healthy lifestyle and eating habits instead of trying to follow some fad diet. Losing weight turned out to be a byproduct of becoming *gone with the sugar*.

Sherry has written this book to share what worked for her so that others can become *gone with the sugar* and enjoy a healthy life!

www.gonewiththesugar.com

Made in the USA
Monee, IL
17 February 2023

28073135R00096